ON BECOMING A GROUP MEMBER

Personal Growth and Effectiveness in Group Counseling

MUHYIDDIN SHAKOOR

Routledge
Taylor & Francis Group
New York London

Routledge
Taylor & Francis Group
270 Madison Avenue
New York, NY 10016

Routledge
Taylor & Francis Group
27 Church Road
Hove, East Sussex BN3 2FA

© 2010 by Taylor and Francis Group, LLC
Routledge is an imprint of Taylor & Francis Group, an Informa business

Printed in the United States of America on acid-free paper
10 9 8 7 6 5 4 3 2 1

International Standard Book Number: 978-0-415-96522-4 (Paperback)

For permission to photocopy or use material electronically from this work, please access www.copyright.com (http://www.copyright.com/) or contact the Copyright Clearance Center, Inc. (CCC), 222 Rosewood Drive, Danvers, MA 01923, 978-750-8400. CCC is a not-for-profit organization that provides licenses and registration for a variety of users. For organizations that have been granted a photocopy license by the CCC, a separate system of payment has been arranged.

Trademark Notice: Product or corporate names may be trademarks or registered trademarks, and are used only for identification and explanation without intent to infringe.

Library of Congress Cataloging-in-Publication Data

Shakoor, Muhyiddin.
   On becoming a group member : personal growth and effectiveness in group counseling / Muhyiddin Shakoor.
      p. cm.
   Includes bibliographical references and index.
   ISBN 978-0-415-96522-4 (pbk. : alk. paper)
   1. Group counseling. 2. Interpersonal communication. I. Title.

BF636.7.G76S43 2010
158'.35--dc22
                                                                           2009030083

Visit the Taylor & Francis Web site at
http://www.taylorandfrancis.com

and the Routledge Web site at
http://www.routledgementalhealth.com

In loving memory of Dr. Virginia P. Harvey, my graduate school professor and mentor, who introduced me to small group studies, to the psychology of group dynamics, and organization change

Contents

Preface · vii
Acknowledgments · ix
Introduction · xi
Orientation Prologue · xiii
Orientation Glossary · xxxv

Group Stages Introduction · 1

1 Beginning Stage · 7

2 Early Middle Stage · 19

3 Late Middle Stage · 39

4 Ending Stage (Termination) · 61

5 Leaders and Group Leadership · 83

6 A Word on Ethical Concerns · 95

Appendix A: Group Member Guide Sheet · 99

Appendix B: Additional Multicultural Resources · 101

Appendix C: Focal Conflict Theory · 103

Appendix D: Helms's Concept of Racial Identity · 107

Appendix E: Table E.1 · 109

Appendix F: Table F.1 · 111

Appendix G: Table G.1 · 113

References	115
Index	123

Preface

My hope is that this book will be of practical use to you the reader, as someone who is presently a group participant or about to enter one of the many different kinds of groups that exist today. The book is intended to serve as a manual that will provide you with an orientation to the general landscape of group work, together with insights into the challenges and opportunities of participation from the group member's point of view. Further, the hope is that the book will assist you in finding ways to be your most effective self within the group. It is an invitation to exploring ways of being in a group that are creative, empowering, self-renewing, and flowing out of your own personhood or center.

Primarily, the book is directed toward readers who are participants in an experiential or counseling group as part of a training program for counseling, psychology, social work, or other helping professions. The book is also intended to be useful for persons entering group therapy or who have been referred to a group for other kinds of support. Some of the suggestions that follow in the prologue are applicable to other types of groups. These may include psychoeducational groups that focus on educating participants, and also groups in corporate settings more oriented toward completing work, formal tasks, and team assignments.

Though the objective of this book encourages a perspective on group participation that is fundamentally grounded in self-awareness, the book also embraces the energy-driven, interactive, and interpersonal aspects of groups that if left unconsidered would cause the book to miss its mark. The kind of development sought for here is one that synthesizes self-knowledge, interpersonal experience, and dynamic ways of being.

Acknowledgments

Many supported the materialization of this little book. I am thankful to my Creator for the life and breath to complete it; to my family for belief in the project, for loving hands-on help in editing, critiquing, listening to scenarios, and keeping patience with me during the days and hours I stowed away in my dungeon, putting words to paper. I owe a special debt of gratitude to Chad Scott, my friend and former student who was my dedicated research assistant, sounding board, and devoted helper. Huge thanks to Yaqub Zimmerman for his help with the design and rendering of figures. I thank the Waterport Community and friends around the world who held off calling so I could get the work done. I thank my departmental colleagues and allies around the College at Brockport and Chi Sigma Iota as well. I thank Ginny Harvey, Jack Gibb, Chris Argyris, and Ibn Arabi for their examples as committed group practitioners and writers. I thank my good friend Craig Waleed for his exquisite editing, vision, and moral support. Special thanks to Jaime Eveland for her insightful remark during our Self-in-Society group of Spring 2002. Also, I thank each and every Brockport student who valued the manuscript when they only had a fragment of what was yet to come. I thank my tenacious agent, Stan Wakefield; my editor, Dana Bliss, who understood my vision; and my reviewers Jim Trotzer and George McMahon. Heartfelt thanks to everyone, including behind-the-scenes people at Taylor & Francis who labored on behalf of a high-quality final product. If you are an unacknowledged angel, I thank you as well. Please forgive my oversight.

"That is a good book which is opened with expectation and closed with profit."

Amos Bronson Alcott
1799–1888

Introduction

SELF: THE FINAL FRONTIER

The extraordinary but elusive entity known as the human self is one of the most central concepts in the helping professions. In spite of its fundamental importance, it remains misunderstood and inadequately pursued. Like an ocean, the regions of self continue to be incredibly vast, amazing, and largely uncharted.

If you were to consider the population of human beings, relating to the self as if it were an ocean, indeed many would be like spectators standing on the shore. Some might wander near to watch the waves and skip a stone or two. A lesser number might remove their shoes and get their feet wet. Fewer would wade out up to their knees and fewer still might swim. A smaller percentage of this few might venture out on a boat, and only a handful of these might dive from the boat and explore the water's depths. From this handful only one or two might find oysters. Finally, between the two, one might surface empty-handed and the other might return with a pearl. As you enter the group, a good thing to consider is which person you choose to be.

An effective group is a place filled with possibilities for exploration, mutual support, and personal growth. In such a place, you can begin an extraordinary journey across the terrain or through the seascape of your own personal ocean. Aside from the spectacular visions of creatures and stuff of the various regions you will likely encounter, you may potentially discover and reclaim your pearl.

As a scene of the cosmos appears, the narrator at the beginning of the *Star Trek* television series routinely makes his introduction saying: "Space ... the final frontier."

The narrator's words may be true for Captain Kirk—and possibly true for many others, but for some—perhaps for you and a few of those Trekkies who seek greater balance, positive energy, transformational change, and personal freedom in their lives—the final frontier is the self. Rather than something to be pursued "out there," it is something that is before us in the moment now. It is here.

Orientation Prologue

PART 1: KEY COMPONENTS OF AN EFFECTIVE MEMBER MINDSET

Purpose

The purpose of this prologue is to provide you with an orientation to effective small group membership. By *small group*, I mean groups with participant numbers generally ranging from six to twelve members. Such numbers are not meant to be taken as a mandate or absolute rule, but I believe that most experienced group leaders would say that the range is feasible. There are always exceptions, but I think that most members would say that eight is almost ideal and twelve is the maximum.

The aim is to assist you as a prospective member or participant as you begin to think about entering a group. I have called Part 1 "Key Components of an Effective Member Mindset" because I want to present you with some of the broad, foundational ideas at the outset that will help you understand how an effective member understands and thinks about group participation. Over time, if these ideas are well utilized, they can help you to become a successful participant and possibly achieve the things you hope for in the group. This section of the Prologue also informs you about some of the challenges you will likely face. You are not expected to memorize or fully internalize all of the points of either part of the Prologue in one reading. In fact, the book is designed in such a way as to invite you to return to review the ideas of the Prologue, Parts 1 and 2, over and over again.

Understand the Purpose of the Group   Understanding the purpose of the group that you are about to enter is an important preparatory step. I encourage you to ask yourself what you understand to be the purpose of the group you are about to enter. If this group experience is your first, or one of few you may have had, it is possible that you are entering with some uncertainty about what will happen. If you have had other group experiences, you may be coming with impressions based on how things were for you at that time. Do you feel ready to start at this time? At the very least, are you willing to begin this self-discovery process?

Entering a group for personal growth or other reasons can sometimes create anxiety, especially if it feels like you are entering unknown territory and you do not know what to expect. Understand that this is normal. If your group has members from diverse ethnic, racial, or cultural backgrounds, understand that discussion and interaction around issues related to these aspects can be highly emotionally charged. If your group is a counseling, psychoeducational, or therapy group, you are probably already aware that you will be interacting and relating with other people in the group. Through the process of interaction, you will have opportunities to gain counseling, self-awareness, and interpersonal communications skills through the activities of the group. You will have many opportunities to discover things about yourself in terms of what your strengths are in your relations with others and what the impacts of your particular style of communication are. You are also likely to discover things about your personal power as well as about your fears. You'll have a chance to acquire strategies for dealing with challenges and crises in your life, for being more productive in situations of conflict, and for fostering growth and positive change in others. It may be helpful to begin thinking of what you would like to achieve or accomplish in the group that may be helpful to you in your life. Consider outlining some goals for yourself that you might begin to look at in the group.

Understand Expectations Relating to Safety

You can expect to be safe in the group. You have a right to expect not to be physically harmed and you should understand that if you threaten the physical safety of others, you will be removed from the group. Neither the group leader nor any other member should attempt to force entry into your private life or deeply personal thoughts. You can expect not to be browbeaten, berated, or ordered to disclose. You have a right to expect a level of respect and freedom to choose. Such a right and expectation, with regard to safety, respect, and freedom, applies to every member. You also have a right to expect group members and the leader to honor the confidentiality of what you share in the group. Likewise, you bear a responsibility to keep the confidentiality of what you hear from others. Understand that failed and violated confidentiality can be a major trust-breaker in a group. Usually, this occurs by subgrouping, in which case one or more group members discuss things shared in the group in outside conversations. Such violations may also include exchanges by telephone and e-mail. Confidentiality in this sense deals with the matter of boundaries in the group as they relate to information flow. Repeatedly, you must make intentional choices regarding information coming to you as well as that which you permit to go out. You will have to consciously manage what you transmit and receive. In other words, you must actively decide when to increase or reduce what information you send out and when and how much to receive of information coming to you. A similar challenge exists for other members in the group. Here the challenge and responsibility are one for both you as an individual participant and for the collectivity of members who compose the group. Kline (2003) utilizes the term *boundarying* as coined by Durkin (1981) to describe this challenge in groups. Further, Kline says "Boundarying implies that individual members have the necessary resources to open their boundaries to receive information and close them to consolidate their learning or protect themselves. Boundary functioning depends on the choices members make to open or close their boundaries" (p. 88). Matters of transmission, reception, and boundaries also relate to the key issue of feedback, which is discussed later in Part 2 of the Prologue.

Check Your Attitude A thoughtful assessment of your frame of mind and attitude as you enter the group is essential. This is especially true in the case of counseling and therapy groups, experiential groups for growth and support, psycho-educational groups, and for some task-oriented groups. Beginning your assessment with a bit of self-reflection, personal inventory, and information can increase your sense of confidence at the outset. The assessment can also help you know that you are in the right place with a better possibility of realizing meaningful gains for the time and effort you spend in the group. This is especially so in the case of therapy, counseling, and personal-growth groups. Sometimes, when these kinds of groups are formed, it is the group leader's responsibility to invite or select members who are appropriate for the group and screen out those who are not good candidates. If you as a prospective member of a group are invited to a screening or preliminary group session, it can be a win–win situation. It makes things better all around if you want to be in the group and have a good attitude about the possibilities of getting something positive for yourself. In some cases, particularly in certain institutions and facilities, screening is not always possible. But here, the main idea is that wherever you are, your attitude and awareness can help you to make a good start.

Asking yourself if you are interested in being in the group is a good first question. In other words, is it your choice to come to the group? Have you been mandated or required to attend for some personal or health-related reason? If you did not choose to come, you may still decide how you want to use your time in the group. If you are coming in with the feeling of being forced, it may still be helpful to acknowledge your unwillingness, lack of interest, or resistance and attempt to reframe it. The ability to shift and flex can be a tremendous personal asset. In other words, it might be helpful to try using your unwillingness to your own advantage and to the group's as well.

Even if you happen to be an unwilling participant, your case is not a lost cause. It can be exceptionally helpful to be aware of how and what you feel. It may be helpful to understand that your personal feelings and reactions can be keys to your effectiveness. I invite you to make a conscious choice to notice them and use them constructively in the group. In other words, after noticing, when you are ready, share your thoughts and say what you feel in the group.

If you are entering the group because you are genuinely interested in discovering more about yourself, you are interested in how to deal with the unique challenges of your life and circumstances, and you are also interested to know more about how others see you, that will make it all the better. It will be easier to have a more positive experience than if you are entering the situation feeling forced.

Other helpful things you might ask yourself are: How willing am I to explore and get to know others? How willing am I to let others get to know me for the purpose of self-improvement? How willing am I to form meaningful connections with others? What do I know about my own personality in terms of my fears and expectations in relationships? What ideas do I have about how I fit in with others? Do I believe that I can truly belong? How do I relate to people who I experience as more powerful or less powerful than myself? What examples stand out in my memory? When I hear the word intimacy or think of feeling close to others, what thoughts come to mind? What happens in my body? What "baggage" do I harbor?

In other words, what do you think impedes your progress in terms of relating to others? Are you able to "take ownership," which means to accept responsibility for what is your own thought, feeling, or impact on others? Are you able to "own" the impact of your choices even on yourself? Do you have experience with trust being broken or painful things of the past that are hard to live with? What ideas do you have at this time about what has to happen in order for you to make peace with your past? By this, I do not mean to necessarily imply that you must "get over it" but rather I mean to ask you to consider how you might come to live your life more fully in spite of your loss or your pain.

Checking personal attitude means thinking through ideas like those mentioned previously and bringing the answers more to the forefront of your awareness as you prepare to enter a group. The attitude that you bring into a group is also a factor in shaping your experience in the group. Along a continuum, your attitude may range from being more facilitative to less facilitative. That is to say that by degrees, your attitude can cause you to be more or less productive.

The more facilitative your attitude is, the more likely it will lead you to productive experiences that foster growth in the group. The less facilitative your attitude is, the more likely it will lead you to counterproductive experiences. A member with a *facilitative* attitude is open to listening, sharing thoughts and feelings, and relating to the experiences of others. A member with a *nonfacilitative* attitude is closed off by choice and not ready to make interpersonal connections.

It is very likely that experiences in the group will explore the types of ideas and themes mentioned previously. Briefly, they include how you relate to others and how you feel about yourself in terms of what you see as your strengths and what areas you see as needing improvement. Also, how you deal with accepting support, friendship, and closeness from others versus being strong, alone, and independent. Other themes touch on challenges you face and goals you have for your life.

If you see that you are absolutely unwilling to enter into this kind of exploration before you enter a group, it is very likely that you are not ready to be an effective group member. In most groups, either directly or indirectly, you will be encouraged to seek an answer to the question "Why am I here?" If the answer is not facilitating your more active interpersonal involvement in the group, you are encouraged to discover new reasons for why you have come. These may include considerations such as: Perhaps, I can discover more about my own potential in spite of my fears. Perhaps, I can risk being known and loved without losing myself or being rejected. Perhaps, I can know the feeling of being worthy, valued, and accepted even if I am not perfect.

Even though ideas and themes may evolve naturally as topics in the group, the objective is not to establish an agenda for group discussion. Rather, the challenge or "work" to be done is to remain aware of yourself in the present moment and time. Remaining aware of yourself includes noticing your thoughts, noticing your feelings and bodily reactions, and possibly even noticing your silence or lack of reaction to what other members (including the leader) say and do. As group members live and explore together, you can make facilitative contributions by sharing your reactions, feelings, and discoveries with others as you notice them coming up here and now.

Open Yourself to Discovery   Openness is a valued member quality in individual counseling and group work.

It can be surprising and challenging to face this expectation in a group because it goes against many prevalent societal norms that encourage and support being superficial. *Openness* refers to your personal accessibility, meaning the extent to which you are willing to let others see who you truly are. This includes the extent to which you are willing to share, reveal, or disclose what you believe, fear, feel, or hope for; what you want or need; what you do well or poorly; and what you like or dislike about yourself. Also relevant is the extent to which you are willing to let others know you, in terms of sharing some of the feelings, thoughts, and attitudes you hold about others.

The cultivation of openness among members of a group can greatly help in reducing defensiveness and developing trust (Bennis & Shepard, 1956; Gibb, 1961; Yalom, 1995). Trust is also identified by Donigian and Malnati (1997) as one of several important issues that are often embedded in group interaction that can be recognized as *themes* that hold potential to unify the group. Openness also improves possibilities for increased self-awareness and discovery because it clears channels for receiving information. More specifically, this means feedback in terms of feelings and reactions from others about how they are experiencing you. This may also include feedback about how they feel about your way of relating as well as feedback about who they think you are. It is also important to understand that you are not expected to be completely vulnerable or helpless in the group. It is not openness at any cost. Rather, it is what I like to think of as *constructive* openness. Occasionally, people who are new to groups enter with the mistaken idea that if they do not weep profusely or disclose the most deep and dark secret of their lives, they are not doing the work of the group. Yes, self-disclosure is essential, but how much you risk or share, examine, or disclose is a developmental process. It is up to you to find your readiness to do it. Tears are acceptable, if they are honest. Deep sharing is acceptable too, but neither of these is a primary objective or goal of group work.

A Few Words About the Johari Window   In speaking about openness, I think that I would be remiss if I do not mention the Johari Window of Joseph Luft (1969). The Johari Window is a model of interpersonal behavior and awareness mapped out in a four-squared matrix that looks like a portrait-oriented window of four panes. Each pane describes aspects of your awareness or lack of awareness with regard to your personal feelings, behaviors, and motivations, when you are alone and also when you are with others.

Moving from left to right, the top quadrants are referred to by Luft as Q-1 and Q-2, which are the Open and Blind quadrants, respectively. Below from left to right are Q-3 and Q-4, the Hidden and Unknown quadrants. Do not panic here if you don't like the combination of numbers and letters or you haven't heard of it before; it is really quite easy once you see it (see Figure P.1).

Luft describes the first quadrant as the area of free activity that contains things that you are aware of about yourself that everyone else can see. Luft's description is partly what made me decide to include it here. He says that "the open quadrant is

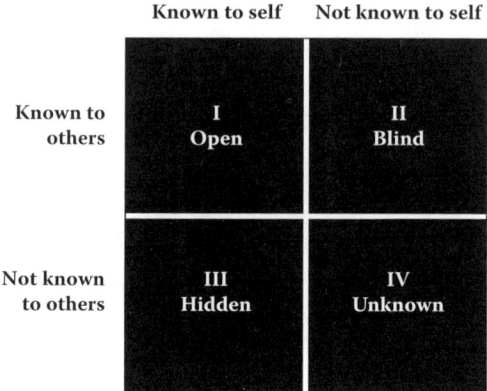

Figure P.1 Johari Window. (From Luft, J., *Of Human Interaction*, New York: McGraw Hill, 1969, p. 13. With permission.)

a window raised on the world—including the self" (p. 14). It includes those behaviors, feelings, motivations, and reactions that are "known to you and to others" that are foundational to interaction and exchange because they are mutually understood. With regard to awareness, the main idea is, as Luft says, "that we all wear masks … and it is equally well-known that we are at times painfully transparent, despite the effort to hide" (p. 19). The stage is set for the "drama of human interaction," says Luft, by the qualities we carry, the need to cover up, and the inescapable possibility of something slipping out or our "inadvertent disclosure" (p. 19). Your challenge in Q-1 is to pick up the challenge of enlarging the quadrant.

Quadrant 2 is the blind area. It refers to those areas of yourself, your feelings, behaviors, motivations, and reactions, that are "known to others but not known to self" (Luft, 1969, p. 13). Here you face the fact that there are aspects of yourself that you do not know that others see very clearly. In group interaction, this quadrant deals with the risks and possibilities of feedback. The question is whether or not you can open yourself to the discovery, to the possibility of knowing, and can you do it without harming others or yourself?

Quadrant 3 is the area of aspects hidden in you but not hidden to you. It is that aspect containing feelings, behaviors, motivations, and reactions that are "known to self but not known to others" (Luft, 1969, p. 13). The hidden quadrant is the private realm. It contains those things in your consciousness that you interact with alone. Luft says that "we carry each other around in our heads and continue in interaction even after the person is not present" (1969, p. 34). Luft also discusses "anticipatory" and "imaginary" interactions where you might interact with the other in your head in preparation for an exchange or create scenes in your own mind with your own ideas of how they may play out. The main idea for this quadrant is that when you choose to disclose your feelings, behaviors, motivations, and reactions, you create expansion. The other person sees more of you "in the open" and your Q-1 becomes larger and more open. Often what comes into the open may include some of what was blind to you before. Disclosures from Q-3 help you to be seen more clearly and leave you with less to hide.

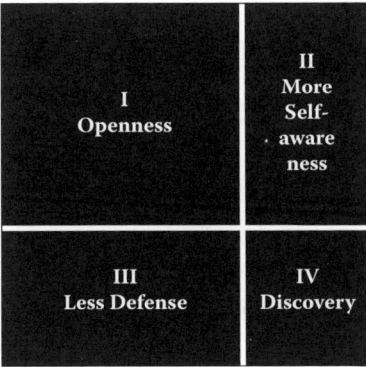

Figure P.2 Johari Window. From Luft, J., *Of Human Interaction*, New York: McGraw Hill, 1969. With permission.)

Quadrant 4 is the unknown area. It is that aspect that contains feelings, behavior, motivations, and reactions that are "not known to self and not known to others" (Luft, 1969, p. 13). Luft says that "interpersonal experiences in a group are enormously complicated by realization of the existence of an unknown area" (1969, p. 64). As you move through the stages of the group you will have an opportunity to increase your awareness of your quadrant 4. As much as it may be horrifying to come to see things in yourself that you or no one else knew existed, of possible past hurt or loss or trauma, there is also the possibility of tapping new resources, new power, latent potential, and new opportunities.

Each quadrant has its challenges and opportunities. Quadrant 1 offers the possibility of increased openness to life and to others. It offers possibilities for increased self-awareness, self-acceptance, and balance in the world with self and others. Quadrant 2 offers the possibility for increased self-awareness by increasing the span of your awareness and reducing what is blind to yourself through interaction with others. Quadrant 3 offers the possibility of reducing defensiveness. When you feel free to show more of what you feel and how you react, you have less to hide and less to protect, but as I have said, the aim is constructive openness, not openness at any cost (see Figure P.2).

In light of these ideas put forth by Luft, together with other great thinkers mentioned in the references for this book, the exploration through initiatives of risk or sharing, examination, or disclosure holds the possibility for increased self-knowledge, discovery, insight, and liberation from the grip of unresolved past personal history. Deep discovery and realization can lead not only to change, but to transformative growth. By *transformative* growth, I mean an extraordinary kind of renewal that may not have seemed possible before. But when its possibility does arrive, an opportunity comes with it for you to become a newer, stronger, more enlightened you. Out of the ashes of who you were, the newer, transformed you rises up like a phoenix. Constructive openness involves risks and benefits. You are continuously choosing and taking chances one moment at a time. Understanding more about the impact of your presence and personality, power, weaknesses, and strengths, about your lovability and talent, is the kind of discovery that groups have to offer. Constructive change and positive ideas about your potential, abilities, and worth can open completely new and unexpected avenues and possibilities in your life.

Understand That Experiential Learning May Be Different From What You Ordinarily Expect in the Classroom or in a Course

In experiential learning settings, effective participants discover that the answers do not necessarily have to come from the leader, teacher, or person in charge. In fact, one key difference in experiential learning settings like personal-growth groups is that the only real answers must come from group members themselves. Often people who are new to experiential group settings find that what is to be learned sometimes is not clear. In other words, ambiguity is high. If you close yourself off to the challenge of continuing to make an effort in moments of ambiguity, you may close yourself off from an opportunity to discover or learn. The experiential concept of "learning how to learn" (Bradford, Gibb, & Benne, 1964) also includes understanding your relationship to other members of the group. Generally, in learning situations, the teacher or leader is the only "teacher." In experiential settings, the teacher may be any member of the group. In experiential groups you have multiple teachers. Each member in the group has at least one thing to offer you that you do not have, which is his or her perception and experience of you. Subsequently, you have multiple resources for discovery and new learning.

Occasionally, a group member may find it difficult to accept that his or her peer may be a potential teacher. At this point the openness challenge emerges again for some group members. If you are one of them, your challenge is to overcome the inclination to devalue the worth of your peers. It may be helpful to consider that the other person likely knows more about his or her own personal reactions and feelings about any member than anyone else. If you are genuinely interested in learning, it behooves you to actively seek to discover what reactions and feelings other members hold about how and who you are.

Understand That Not Having Perfect Clarity and Being Uncomfortable Are Okay

Tolerance for ambiguity and maintaining inner balance during moments of uncertainty or when clear direction is lacking are other keys to effective participation in groups. Most human beings appreciate understanding what the rules and expectations are when entering new situations. In group work, this expectation is referred to as "need for structure." Need for structure relates directly to member orientations toward authority, which are addressed later in Chapter 1. However, a point of interest here about group members in this regard is that the individuals who compose the group may be very similar or differ greatly in how much structure they "need" in order to feel comfortable. Effective group membership requires that you examine your need for structure and your expectations to be comfortable. In the group it is more helpful to think that "you must take chances in order to be comfortable rather than to think that you must be comfortable before you take chances" (J. Eveland, personal communication, April 2002).

A key to your effective participation, which is critically important here, is that you remain alert in the face of disempowering fear that may arise from uncertainty and discomfort. I invite you to make a growth-supporting choice. Foster the will and capacity within yourself to continue making an effort in the group, even when you feel uncomfortable or when things are not perfectly clear. Understand that your effective participation may require personal change. Such change may involve shifting your way of thinking about yourself or others. It may require that you adjust your definition of what you believe is a need to a desire or a preference. It may also require change in terms of how you address feelings, in deeply personal ways within yourself or more generally in terms of how you relate to others. Carl Rogers (1969) says it well: "All significant learning is to some degree painful and involves turbulence, within the individual and within the system" (p. 157). You may wonder what kind of change is being pursued here. Understand that I am not advocating for pain per se or suggesting that you must like it. Rather, I am suggesting that you consider not being deterred from things you want or hope for, for fear of having to deal with discomfort. You may wonder what kind of change is worth having pain and discomfort. You may wonder if the change that is referred to here is only another prescription for temporary change that will be here only for a moment. But what I refer to is lasting personal change and how it can be cultivated and fostered in you. Such cultivation as this requires noticing, acknowledgment, and willingness. *Noticing* means becoming aware of what is out of balance in yourself or in your life. *Acknowledgment* refers to ownership, meaning that you accept responsibility for the problem or issue that is here and now, present inside of you and in your life, regardless of how it got here. *Willingness* means your openness to experiment with different ways of viewing your world. If you come to see that your way of looking has not borne the fruits you hoped for, perhaps it is time to face the fact that the fruits are not really there. Perhaps it is also time to reassess your outlook, especially with regard to how you believe change and growth happen. Are you someone who is most often changed by unexpected, surprising things that come up in your life in terms of people or events? In other words, when you look honestly at your locus of control, would you say it is internal or external? If you knew that shifting toward or more strongly emphasizing or establishing an internal locus of control could help you to obtain the fruits you hope for, would you be willing to look more closely at where you are along the line that runs between the two?

Group participation has great potential to facilitate such kinds of assessment, exploration, shifts, or affirmation. If you are a member with a genuine interest in growth, you may be empowered by the value the group environment places upon self-awareness, interpersonal relationships, the impact of social learning, and the role and power of feedback in changing human behavior.

Keep in Mind the Interactive Processes of Group Work
The central focus of group work is interpersonal. In other words, several people are together as group members and the focus is on what happens among and between them. The various levels of energy, force, and impact or lack of such that characterize the feeling of interactions among people in the group are known as *dynamics*. Donigian and Malnati (1997) describe the group as a *three-element system*. Their view is that every therapy group consists of three elements: the member, the leader, and the group. Each element is considered to be essential to effective group work, but the

real attention is on how transactions are exchanged among these elements of the group. Kline (2003) has named his text *Interactive Group Counseling and Therapy*, in which he acknowledges what he calls <u>core interpersonal issues</u> that are presented in most classic group development theories. These interpersonal issues, which include involvement, dependency, authority, individuation, intimacy, and loss, represent the core of a group development schema. The issue confronted by the group at any particular time denotes the group's stage of development. An effective group member notices which issues and related themes are most prevalent in the group's interaction. Your awareness of these issues will provide insights into the interactive and dynamic nature of groups. Therefore, it is important that you actively attempt to observe what happens between yourself and other group members. It is helpful to notice what happens between yourself and the group leader, what happens between yourself and the group, and what happens to you within the context of the group as a unit or system.

When you interact with others in the group while remaining aware of these three elements, you can experience the nature of their interdependence. Further, you can actually see the relationship of yourself to the group and its members. You may also gain a glimpse into how it feels to experience the group as a living social system. Awareness of the three elements considered together with the three qualifying steps opens the possibility of seeing yourself and others more clearly. In fact, Hulse-Killacky (2001) identifies three questions that will propel group members to greater involvement if they are honestly explored: Who am I? Who am I with you? and Who are we together? (p. 9).

Learn How to Think in Process Terms and Distinguish Between Content and Process
In group work, <u>content</u> refers to the apparent topic or activity. For example, if a group member who is a widow tells the group about her first date before getting married, the content will be the words of her story. Content is usually experienced in degrees of density while at the same time remaining external, obvious, and, for the most part, on the surface. Matters relating to content are likely to be visible or audible or both. The substance of this content may be perceived as negative, positive, or indifferent.

<u>*Process*</u> refers to the less obvious energy or feeling that accompanies the content. In the case of the widow's story, examples of process might be a feeling of warmth or even of anger or pain surfacing in the group as the story is told. It could also be that for the widow the process aspect is anguish, whereas for the group it is frustration because the story may have been told once or twice before. Process is the animating principle of groups. It is usually experienced in degrees of intensity and energy that affect the quality of feeling in group interaction. Usually, matters relating to process are not visible or audible but they are noticeable and clearly felt. Nonfacilitative members' attitudes and feelings, including resistance to participate, boredom, or lack of interest are examples of process-level concerns.

Content is distinguished by observable behavior that gives hints or clues about the existence of nonfacilitative attitudes. Examples might be such things as responses to questions with silence, distracting comments expressed by group members during sessions, repeated verbal expressions of confusion, or demands for increased leader help to the group.

Content and process are a unity of two elements interacting with each other. In group situations, they are always present together. In the context of interpersonal relationships, content and process usually occur simultaneously over a designated period of time. The following guide may help you to understand which is which in the group. Your answer to the question, "What is happening in the group?" will likely identify something related to content. Your answer to the questions: "How are things happening in this group?" and "What is the feeling/tone that accompanies 'the what'?" will likely identify something related to process. It may be helpful for you to think of content and process as two sides of one coin. So as an effective member, you are encouraged to develop the ability to notice what is happening in one or another of the dimensions or simultaneously in both.

In effective groups where content and process are in balance, group members experience the group as inherently more dynamic and alive regardless of the nature of themes or topics. In other words, process is the activating cause of meaningful and facilitative interaction in groups. When groups are experienced as flat, slow-moving, and lacking energy, the explanation usually has to do with process.

Understanding the subtle relationship between content and process is one of most important challenges of group work. More than any other effectiveness-related challenge, achieving an integrated understanding of the interaction between content and process will likely do the most to move you as a group-work apprentice to a level of mastery that few participants ever achieve.

Develop the Capacity to Handle Conflict and Confrontation

Successful growth groups almost always experience conflict. Conflict may be *intrapersonal*, meaning that it is internal to yourself, or *interpersonal*, which means that it is between you and one or more other people. Experiential learning settings encourage interpersonal contact that immediately forces members into greater awareness of their boundaries. For this reason, conflict in groups may happen simultaneously on more than one level.

As a participant in any group, the mere fact of being placed in proximity to others will bring challenges related to intimacy and authority. *Intimacy* refers to how you deal with closeness in relationships and *authority* refers to how you deal with others whom you experience as powerful (Bennis & Shepard, 1970). Privately held expectations about the extent to which your hopes will be realized or crushed lead to collective challenges for the group as a unit and will likely bring your own issues and those of others to the surface.

If you hope to be a group member who deals effectively with conflict, it will be important that you acquire the following essential abilities and skills. These include

1. The ability to tolerate being uncomfortable.
2. The ability to remember to notice your own thoughts, feelings, and reactions to others in the moment they are happening. Particularly important are your "hopes" for yourself in the group, awareness of fears you have about your hopes, and "predictions" you have about what your end result will be.

3. Willingness and ability to express your feelings and risk letting others know something of your fears, hopes, and expectations of yourself as well as those you have of others.[1]
4. The ability to listen and reflect.
5. The ability to convey and receive constructive feedback.

As you grow and increase your effectiveness as a group member, it is likely that you will not only acquire the previously mentioned skills, but also that you will acquire an ability to utilize the skills in synthesis and with facility. For further insights on conflict see Appendix C.

Cultivate Conditions Within That Foster Growth for Yourself and Others An effective group participant is always seeking balance between his or her own inner-focused development and relationships with others in the group. Individuals who grasp the significance of this process develop attitudes and ways of being within that have an observable impact in their activity, initiatives, and contact with others in the group. Reflect on what follows.

Consider your inner self as a garden and your relationships with others as fruit and flowers. When you do this, you can see that the quality of your produce will be directly linked to how you cultivate your garden. Establishing what Rogers (1957) describes as "necessary and sufficient conditions" is like spreading rich fertilizer into the soil and also having plenty of water and sunshine (p. 95). With all of these things present, barring something unforeseen, it is very likely that something beautiful will grow.

The necessary conditions are attitudes that show something of what your garden is like. They also teach you how your way of being causes the gardens of others to falter or flourish when they come into contact with you. A facilitative, growth-engendering attitude reflects three qualities. Namely, these are congruence, empathy, and unconditional positive regard (Rogers, 1957).

Congruence When you are congruent, others experience you as real or genuine. You do not hide behind roles and false personas. Others experience that who you truly are inside yourself is who you present naturally and honestly as you interact with others.

Empathy When you are empathic, other people experience your care. When you are empathic, you attempt to get a sense of the inner world and inner experience of others. They feel your interest to understand them and to understand their feelings. You grapple with establishing the unique but always shifting "dynamic balance" of being deeply involved with others, but not overinvolved and simultaneously detached but not aloof.

Unconditional Positive Regard When you possess this unconditional positive regard, you find an increasing capacity within yourself to accept the total being of others without judgment or qualification. You are able to be with others without interpreting or evaluating their feelings. What is more, you remain at ease in this attitude regardless of what the other member says or does. Even if the other member engages in behavior that is inappropriate or counterproductive, that person remains accepted even if the behavior is not.

Choose to Become a Group Work Apprentice Becoming an effective group member is similar to becoming an apprentice. An apprentice is a person who is interested in achieving mastery in his or her field of pursuit. *Mastery* refers to a level of development where skill, knowledge, and experience flow together with who you are as a person. This "flowing together" is commonly referred to as *integration*. Any apprentice seeking mastery must qualify for entering apprenticeship by three steps we have mentioned before: interest, openness to discovery, and willingness to change. If you have these qualities, you can begin. After you begin, you must negotiate the lessons and challenges faced by apprentices of the past and bring the outcomes and insights of the learning process into your current awareness and presently lived experience. In other words, in group work a qualified apprentice's experience in the group draws him or her through a journey that provides possibilities for dynamic insight and growth. The extent to which the apprentice achieves insight, growth, and later integration corresponds directly to the level of investment or dedication to the qualifying steps above.

In the books of Carlos Castaneda (1972), his teacher Don Juan clearly outlines the challenges to an apprentice on the sorcerer's path, which parallel those of group work. The foremost of these is what Carlos's teacher refers to as "changing one's idea of the world" (1972, p. 313). The three-step qualification set forth earlier is an expansion of the one set forth by Castaneda. As you enter the journey or group work process, you may begin to see how incredibly vast your scope of awareness can be. You may see how complex and surprising human beings are, and how much you can even come to know about yourself ... beyond your present limitations. The member who chooses to enter the group work apprenticeship opens him- or herself to the possibility of seeing that things are not as they seem. Most often it seems that when humans assess their or another's potential they are inclined to underestimate. Sometimes you discover that neither you nor the other is as you thought they were.

PART 2: BASIC STRATEGIES AND SKILLS FOR SUCCESSFUL INVOLVEMENT IN THE GROUP

Purpose

The purpose of Part 2 of the Prologue is to further assist in your orientation to effective small group membership. I have called Part 2 "Basic Strategies and Skills for Successful Involvement in the Group" because the skills described here are fundamental, widely utilized, and widely agreed upon as essentially important to effective group membership and participation. Again, you are not expected to memorize or fully internalize all of the points but rather to attempt to apply them to the scenarios and to your live group as well. You are encouraged to return to the Prologue and its ideas as often as you like.

Be Here. Be Now These four seemingly small words have had a colorful history and powerful impact on contemporary psychology, culture, learning, and social thought (Dass, 1971; Rank, 1936; Rogers, 1961; Tolle, 1999). Having been extracted from the wisdom of non-Western thinkers often by Western seekers in pursuit of meaning in their lives, for some the injunction "Be Here Now" has almost become a cliché in spite of its exceptional importance. Understanding what "being here and being now" means is very likely one of the foremost facilitators of effective involvement in group work (Bennis & Shepard, 1956; Bradford, Gibb, & Benne, 1964; Corey, M.S. & Corey, G., 1977; Donigian & Malnati, 1997; Golembiewski & Blumberg, 1970; Kline, 2003; Luft, 1969; Rogers, 1970; Yalom, Lieberman, & Miles, 1973). It is my view that in the process of becoming an effective group member, when you are genuinely interested in growth, you will notice in yourself and in other group members a subtle shift from concerns about what to do to concern about how to be. When you become a member who participates from the "being" mode, most often you and others will experience you as more energetic and alive. "Being-mode" energy is observable when expressed through bodily action and speech within the context of certain interactions in the group.

Similarly, in an effective growth group, greater emphasis is placed on the present time and less on the past and future. For insight into the extent to which you are not in the present, you need only take a moment to notice the trend of your own thoughts, feelings, and conversation. You may notice that you think and talk about the future—where you hope to be and what you hope to do. You may notice that you think and talk about the past and what you had or where you were before. You may also notice whether you are oriented to the present and where you are today. If you are a carefully observant group member, it is highly probable that you will notice this tendency in other members of the group.

For some, "Be Here Now" is merely a catchword; for others, it is a magnificent golden key. Whether or not the key unlocks and opens the treasure chest depends on the attitude, awareness, and intention of the one who holds it. The extent to which you are able to successfully utilize the key in a group depends on the three things just mentioned and also upon your willingness to grapple with the demands of implementing a paradigm shift that takes you away from the prevalent cultural view of human interaction. Generally, groups for counseling, therapy, or personal growth have a culture that is uniquely their own. Sometimes they include and emphasize things in ways that are exactly as they are in the general culture outside the group. At other times, groups may include and emphasize things that are entirely different from what is generally emphasized outside. Grappling with these differences is part and parcel of the process of your group-work apprenticeship and path to becoming an effective member. In some groups, this challenge is felt to be so powerful and so profound that it is simply not approached and not addressed.

Effective participation in most counseling, therapy, and growth groups encourages taking a step toward discovering what being human truly is. It invites you to explore who you are and what is possible when you feel yourself being at your best. Effective participation involves liberating yourself from ways of meeting others and doing things from a place in you of unspoken but projected expectations, fears, or unconscious needs and desires.

You may use remembering and intention to bring yourself more into the present moment in the group. You simply notice where your attention, feelings, or thoughts are in time and space. If they are not *here*, you may redirect them to the present by quiet reflection or by open speech that acknowledges the thoughts. If they are not *now*, the method is the same. As an effective group participant, you are "always" attempting to remember to notice the "here" and speaking about what is here, about yourself or what is happening between yourself and the other, here. Remembering to notice the now is the same. It is speaking about this moment—this hour, at this time within you, or between you and the other. The effective participant actively chooses the challenge of remaining alert and warding off forgetfulness and fading awareness. Ram Dass (1971) provided group-work apprentices with the same foundational wisdom when he inscribed a string of words that were the secret key to his book around the medallion on its cover: Remember. Be Here Now. Remember. Now Be Here.

Listen and Reflect Skill in listening is basic to effective group participation. Listening refers to your capacity to be still enough to allow another's message to be expressed, acknowledged, and heard. Ideally, the message will be understood if these conditions are met. This is not to say that the sender of the message has no responsibility for part of the communication. It is simply that the focus here is listening.

Listening is a core component of communication, which is in turn fundamentally important to interpersonal relationships. Communication is a complex process that has several components, of which listening is only one. The main idea is that effective communication most often requires two characteristics at the personal level, namely, willingness and ability. These requirements naturally apply to listening because listening is a part of communication. Because earlier we touched upon the sender, parenthetically, let it be said here that the requirements we have just mentioned also apply to the sender. There is also a tenor or spirit of communication that can be facilitative in the communication process. This is an aspect of willingness. It is that both the listener and sender make their best attempt to be honest, forthright, and as clear as possible about what they hope to convey.

Effective communication is highly relevant to group work because it fosters interpersonal contact that helps members to know more about each other. Communication is a key element in structuring relationships. Effective communication has the potential to sustain interpersonal involvement that deepens as members come to better know each other and hopefully later trust each other. This communication and trust among members facilitate the evolution of the group as a cohesive unit.

Reflection is also a part of the communication process. It refers to the ability of the listener to show how and what parts of the speaker's message he or she has heard. By reflection is meant that you actively attend to what is being said as to the content, thoughts, and feelings of the speaker's message. You, then, as the effective listener, reflect back or "mirror" what you have heard the speaker say to you in the words and manner it has been said. You may, after an attempt to reflect a speaker's remarks, inquire as to whether or not your reflection or what you think you have heard is accurate. No other types of questions are appropriate in this particular process. The proper use of reflection can be exceptionally facilitative in the group culture. Reflection is an effective facilitative alternative to asking questions that are often counterproductive. In parts of the general cultural context outside the group, questions are often considered as something valuable. Indeed, questions are vital. However, sometimes in counseling, therapy, and growth groups, a member's question may, in some instances, be more an indirect statement than a query for needed information or request to know something from the other person. In indirect instances, responsibility is sometimes shifted away from the person to whom it belongs onto someone else. Persons who are new to counseling, therapy, and growth groups sometimes struggle with making these idiosyncratic "cultural" shifts.

The tendency to overrely on questions is most often consistently counterproductive in group work and frequently leads to poorly established "norms," which are group guidelines for effective communication. The main objectives of the group-work culture are to foster self-awareness, interpersonal connection, honesty, directness, and personal responsibility. For these reasons, members are encouraged to state their needs and say what they want more directly. It is not that questions are never good, never useful, and absolutely forbidden. It is simply that part of the remembering and awareness challenge for effective group participants is to notice the intent and origin of their questions.

Learn to Convey and Receive Feedback The ability to convey and receive feedback is essential to effective group participation. In order to convey feedback constructively, good observation skills are essential. You must also listen well and be able to reflect back to the speaker in a concise, nonevaluative, and nonjudgmental way what you have heard. It is important to keep your feedback specific and to the point. Immediacy can also be helpful in conveying feedback, meaning that it is related to present or recently noticed behavior or events. In order to receive feedback you must have a receptive attitude and listen well. It also helps if you are able to not take what sometimes feels like criticism personally. Having the capacity to shift, adapt, and maintain a balance between not becoming too detached and aloof but, on the other hand, not becoming too ego-involved is extremely helpful in receiving feedback.

Constructive feedback is focused on behavior. In other words, useful feedback is based on bodily action or speech that can be noticed by anyone in the group. Most especially, the person who is receiving the feedback should be able to see what he or she does that relates to your feedback. If you do not, as the person conveying feedback, internalize the importance of focusing on behavior, you may slip into stating your assessment, evaluation, opinion, judgment, or interpretation. Your interpretation will likely follow with attempts to prove or justify your assessment and in the end be nonfacilitative. Personal evaluation, if there is any, should come after the recipient's behavior is identified. Such interpretation, evaluation, or opinion is most helpful when it is not cast in stone. In other words, your personal evaluation or opinion is most helpful if it is presented as your perceived meaning as an observer and as something that is open to be changed or reconsidered. Personal opinion may or may not be fact. In the group all members will likely be able to agree on what behavior was displayed in the group, but perceptions about what the behavior means may differ widely.

Constructively conveyed feedback has tremendous potential to facilitate and foster increased self-awareness by helping a receptive member to notice aspects of his or her behavior, its impact, and, subsequently, his or her "blind spots." For these reasons, an effective group participant values feedback. In pursuit of effectiveness, it may dawn upon you that each group member has at least one valuable thing to offer. Namely, it is his or her unique and personal perception of you.

Express Feelings as Feelings   The effective expression of feelings requires interest, ability, acquiring a vocabulary of feeling words, and developing a style of interpersonal communication in which feelings are expressed as feelings. You may experience a cultural challenge here because feelings are often expressed as thoughts and vice versa, in general societal communication. However, in group work, *feelings* refer to the domain of affect or emotion-based experience. Expressing feelings effectively in the context of counseling, therapy, and growth groups (and communications-centered partnerships such as marriage) sometimes requires a shift away from how you may express feelings generally in social situations. For example, "I feel that you do not understand me" expresses a thought or belief. An unexpressed feeling may be hidden in the statement. Effectively expressed, it might be: "I feel disappointed because I don't think you understand me."

Acquiring a vocabulary of feeling words requires that you make the distinction between thoughts and feelings and develop a personal "feeling-word" resource. It is a challenging ability to gain because in typical Western culture, we do not communicate so specifically. However, in counseling and therapeutic circumstances, it is more helpful to say "I feel" only when a clear expression of feeling follows using words such as afraid, excited, encouraged, tired, happy, or sad. Most often, statements beginning with "I feel like ..." or "I feel that ..." do not lead to a clear expression of feeling.

Initiate Consistently to Avoid Fading Into Silence   Effective group participation presents new members with the personal challenge of understanding what *initiating* means in group work. Initiating refers to the ability to start, begin, or sustain action in the group. Productive initiatives usually involve original actions on your part. An initiative may be a statement of self-disclosure, expression of a want or need, or a demand for something from another member of the group. Purposeful but nonproductive initiatives do occur. Most often these are characterized by transitional talk about the weather or how one's day went, usually happening throughout group life but mostly at the start of group sessions.

An initiative may be a challenge, confrontation, or an invitation to move, share, stop, accelerate, diminish, or change any aspect of the group. Each member of the group bears the responsibility of learning what effective work is. Such learning supports the establishment of norms that help the group to maintain itself as a successful unit. When group members initiate in the spirit of effective work alone, simultaneously, or in tandem with the initiative of others, the group begins to become dynamic, alive, and productive.

Persons who are new to groups often come with private internally held rules about spontaneity, chaos, and order related to how and when they should speak in a group. Some new members do not speak unless no one else is speaking. Often they are silent regardless of whether someone else is speaking or not. Sometimes, while others are speaking, thoughts or things come to mind that they want to share but do not. These members also report that they fear interrupting or cutting someone off, changing the theme or topic at hand, or being rude.

Growth groups tend to recapitulate or represent experiences members have had in the primary family group (Yalom, 1995). Members often unconsciously behave and react to group members and group situations in ways that mirror how they reacted in their original family groups. Some group members see that they have come to be seen as silent members because they hold themselves back from speaking. Sometimes a silent member comes to see that rules about not speaking and not interrupting were earlier internalized in her or his life at home.

Members who follow these rules in the group usually stop themselves from initiating, bind themselves up in silence and perceived safety, and reduce opportunities for making meaningful contact with others.

Monitor Your Personal Process (Become Familiar With Your Emotional Wiring and Cognitive Mechanics)

Effective and facilitative participation in group work is fundamentally tied to two things: awareness of self and awareness of process. Earlier it was mentioned that process is the animating principle of groups. Your personal process is largely what animates you. Most often, it will include aspects of thinking and feeling. In the context of group work, personal processes refer to your emotional "wiring" and cognitive "mechanics," so to speak.

Emotional wiring has to do with how you operate in terms of feelings or affect. It is how you relate or withdraw when you experience or encounter emotion within yourself or from others. *Cognitive mechanics* describe how you characteristically think and react in nonemotional ways when you relate to others or they relate to you.

Effective participation requires that you develop the ability to notice what you emphasize mentally or emotionally in various situations according to the extent to which you feel comfortable or at ease. Discovering what openness means in personal terms and gauging what feels appropriate in relating to others is a part of the opportunity and challenge of group work. Your personal process is an influential subpart of the group's process. Understanding your own personal process is a key to understanding what makes the group's energy level and feeling quality or atmosphere as it is. Group process is the unified outcome of individual processes, and its whole is greater than the sum of its parts.

Utilize the "Three Lenses" Approach for Practicing the Skills and Staying Involved

The three lenses approach for effective participation refers to a dynamic perspective in which you shift your awareness among three points of view. They are seeing myself, seeing the other, and seeing the group. Each perspective is a lens that holds the possibility of boosting your effectiveness when it is thoughtfully utilized in the group. Your challenge is to remember to notice which lens you are seeing through, risk sharing what you notice, and continually shifting your awareness from lens a to b to c. When you look through the lens, you see where to implement any of the skills reviewed above and make your initiative.

The Seeing Myself Lens When looking through this lens, you see from the perspective of what you experience in yourself in any given moment in the group. This may include unexpressed thoughts; "self-talk," meaning things you say to yourself; and feelings that you notice once you remember to notice but usually do not express. The aim here is to learn to be an objective observer of your own experience.

The Seeing the Other Lens When looking through this lens, you see from the perspective of what you experience in yourself in any given moment as you relate to any other member of the group. Once you remember to notice, you may venture out to share or disclose things like "in this moment this is how I experience you." You may also discover things you feel about your relationship or lack of relationship with the other. You may notice unexpressed hopes or other reactions or experiences that engender the quality of feeling that exists or not between you and the other member.

The Seeing the Group Lens When you look through this lens, you see the group as a whole. You see yourself as a person within the entity of the group. Once you remember to notice, you may share the extent to which you feel attracted to the group and the extent to which you feel accepted in the group. Researchers have found that acceptance and attraction are two key elements relating to psychological membership in groups (Jackson, 1969; Shakoor & Rabinowicz, 1978). You may also notice the "climate" or what the weather of the group is like for you. You may share how you experience the atmosphere of the group environment as cold or warm, supportive or alienating, safe or threatening, or whatever your experience may be.

Track Your Awareness, Discovery, and Learning by Keeping a Journal
Journal-keeping is one of the most useful but underrated personal development tools in experiential learning settings. In any ongoing group, a journal is both fundamental and facilitative because it enables you to gain perspective on yourself and your experience in the group. In fact, keeping a journal puts you into interaction with yourself and provides you with opportunities to get a more objective view of your subjective experiences over time in the group. Tracking success or struggle and keeping a record of how and what you become aware of, discover, and learn help to foster your personal integration. Utilizing skills such as remembering to remember, being here and now, and observing are likely to be useful.

As you develop your record, you bring all of the pieces of your experience together. In some instances, your experience and reactions will be illustrated and elucidated to yourself. In other instances you will have documented things that you have forgotten which can be revisited. The process of recording or documenting your personal experience assists you to be a more effective participant in the following ways: facilitates process, facilitates reflection, facilitates remembering, and facilitates understanding.

1. Facilitates Process: Keeping a journal actually fosters greater observation and involvement in your own personal process. The act of writing involves you in remembering to notice. It also involves you in following what goes on in your affective and cognitive responses as you relate to yourself and others through lenses a, b, and c. Keeping the journal also gives you a chance to see how your personal process impacts group process, particularly in terms of change, "cohesion," or sense of bonding and community spirit.
2. Facilitates Reflection: Keeping a journal provides you with the opportunity to notice what aspects of interaction affect you in personal ways. When you take time to notice what people, activities, or things have touched you the most, writing offers opportunities to reflect on how you feel or think about group events. You have a chance to review your attitude or see what you have worked through or avoided. You have a chance to decide new directions for yourself within the group.
3. Facilitates Remembering: Keeping a journal helps you to remember important things that you would like to avoid forgetting. The journal provides you an opportunity to see exactly how it is that you remember yourself and what you do. The journal gives you the opportunity to revisit "barometric" events or moments when powerful things happened in the group that changed the group members and you. Through remembering you get a chance to see how you have evolved in your sense of what is here and now. You gain a historical view of yourself in terms of where and how you were and how you are now.
4. Facilitates Understanding: Keeping a journal facilitates insight and helps you to understand how you are and what you do within the group. Keeping a journal helps you better understand what group work is about through your personal experience. You see the main interactions for each session that you find the most powerful or instructive, you note the members (including yourself or not) who are involved in the most significant interaction. You make note of themes, topics, and issues that are most prevalent in the group and you may note the extent to which themes and topics reflect your own private thoughts or expressed feelings or reactions. In this way, you gain a vision of yourself, others, and the group as a unit, functioning in some interrelated way. Your ability to see group life in this way will likely give you a sense of confidence that you know increasingly more about what the factors are that make a group effective or not.

Remember to Remember Remembering is a key to successful involvement in group work. Remembering illuminates and sustains awareness. Awareness is a living process that moves multidimensionally in expanding and contracting concentric circles. In other words, awareness is dynamic and it moves in and fades away. You can sustain your awareness of yourself and your thoughts and feelings by remembering to remember how you intend to be and what you hope to do. You may notice that remembering requires a certain level of alertness and effort. Sometimes things of extraordinary significance may slip away and be irretrievably lost because you forget. Productive involvement in a group presents each member with the challenge of shifting his or her personal paradigm toward living more in a state of "remembering to notice."

In the group, opportunities for experimenting and making this paradigm shift come up moment by moment. Well-seized moments and opportunities usually bring rich rewards in terms of increased awareness, powerful interpersonal contact, and a sense of being more truly alive.

Examine Your Intention Intention is a key to successful involvement in group work. It is also fundamental to increased self-awareness and to being here and being now. *Intentionality* refers to the extent to which you consciously choose. It has to do with clarifying your purpose or envisioning the outcome you hope for before you act. It is helpful to examine your intention before entering a group. As your experience and awareness shift and change over time, reexamining your intention may continue to be helpful. Intention is subtle, but like remembering it is also living and dynamic. Intention is also very likely to be a noticeable influence upon the nature of your impact in the group at personal, interpersonal, and whole-group levels. Groups with members who have shared publicly, who are aware of and clearly understand each other's intentions, will likely become more bonded or cohesive.

Intention is not meant to interfere with spontaneity and risk-taking. If you notice that you are not as spontaneous or as risking as you might like to be, examining or reexamining your intention may be a useful thing to do.

Utilizing Prologue Tips After Group Stage Chapters

For your further assistance, I have provided selected "tips" from Parts 1 and 2 of the Orientation Prologues. After each group stage chapter discussion and questions for review, these tips conclude the chapters. The listing of Selected Tips presents points from the Prologues in brief that are relevant for you according to which stage the group is in. They are not intended to be exact science but are simply meant to serve as an encouraging guide and reminder. Hopefully, you will find the tips and the components and skills they refer to helpful and user friendly. Whenever you want to review the Prologue components and strategies more fully, you can easily flip to the front of the text.

Utilizing Appendices

I have included seven appendices, A through G, in addition to a few music resources. Because only Appendices B and C are referenced in the text, I would like to mention the others and say a few words about how they may be used.

Appendix A is a Group Member Guide Sheet that may be used as a personal assessment form that identifies areas of knowledge, skills, and strategies that you have effectively grasped and integrated or, alternatively, which may need continued work on your part in order to maximize your development and effectiveness as a member. Likewise, this form can be utilized as a guide for feedback to other members so that members may conduct assessments of other members and share the points of that assessment according to the guide sheet as constructive feedback about aspects of their participation. Group leaders may utilize the form as an orientation form for members that helps them to see which areas of knowledge, skills, or strategies they should seek to develop in themselves. Leaders may also ask members to conduct a self-assessment using the form and initiate self-reporting on their perceptions of the quality and effectiveness of their participation.

Appendix B lists valuable multicultural resources in the categories of films and books.

Appendix C is a discussion of focal conflict theory that can be useful for both group members and leaders in understanding the dynamics of conflict in interpersonal interactions in groups. This appendix also includes Figure C.1, which illustrates the process of the theory.

Appendices D through G all relate to the racial identity theory of Janet E. Helms. An overview is provided in Appendix D and Appendices E, F, and G each contain tables that provide a summary of racial identity ego statuses and information processing strategies for Whites or a summary of the same for African Americans, Latinos, Asians, and Native Americans. I have included these references to Helms because of the current significance and scope of multicultural concerns for the social professions and Helms's dedicated investigation into multicultural issues and concerns of ethnicity and race. These appendices are considered as introductory. Further investigation into these topics can be pursued after the development of fundamental self-awareness skills applied within the multicultural context.

NOTE

1. Your sense of safety is a factor in the risk you take. Understand that you are not expected to expose yourself to the extent that you feel completely vulnerable and helpless. If you notice that the thought of sharing certain things about yourself brings these feelings, sharing those fears and feelings about things you are not yet ready to disclose could be a meaningful place to start.

Orientation Glossary

Some useful words and terms to know as you begin.

acceptance: A quality by which one or several individuals feel positively received into the group. It is valuable for you as a member to have a sense of being accepted by the group in order to have a meaningful experience.

advice giving: Instructing or providing someone with information or recommendations about what to do in a particular situation. Advice was one of the main techniques of E. G. Williamson (1939) and his directive counseling approach of the 1930s. Advice giving was challenged as a technique by Carl Rogers (1961) because of its tendency to promote client dependency and interfere with the client's growth. Advice is used sparingly in most counseling approaches today. It is employed mainly in crisis situations in which it either prevents clients from engaging in destructive acts or gives clients something beneficial to do when they are not able to generate constructive plans of action because of being overwhelmed by trauma. Advice giving, if not used judiciously, prevents clients from struggling with their own thoughts, feelings, and behaviors (Gladding, 2001).

ALANA: An acronym used by social scientists to refer to people of color including African Americans, Latinos, Asians, and Native Americans.

ambiguity: The characteristic quality of uncertainty in the beginning stages of most groups. It is akin to what people sometimes feel when entering new social situations. Most often the term applies to group members' sense of lacking structure or to an atmosphere of hesitancy in which members' anxieties about what to do in order to be productive is highly prevalent. From the perspective of effective membership, developing the capacity to function effectively in situations that are unclear, uncertain, or ambiguous is considered to be helpful.

anxiety: Mental and physical nervousness and uneasiness, often resulting in increased tension, usually associated with pressure to please, fear of failure, or the unknown. Anxiety may be connected with concrete events or free floating and not attached to any one particular thing (Gladding, 2001).

atmosphere: The group environment or group surroundings and their unique climatic feeling. Developing the ability to consciously notice or discern what the atmosphere of a group is like with regard to its warmth or tension or coldness can support your effectiveness as a member.

attack on the leader: When members of the group become hostile or rebellious in regard to a leader's authority or his or her conducting of the group. Underlying reasons for such attacks are subgrouping, fear of intimacy, and extragroup socializing (Gladding, 2001).

attraction: The second of the two key elements that relate to psychological membership in groups. Attraction is a quality by which one or several individuals feel drawn to the group. It is valuable for you as a member to feel attracted to the group and accepted by the group for the most beneficial experience in the group.

authoritarian leaders: Leaders who envision themselves as experts and retain all decision-making power. These leaders interpret, give advice, and generally direct the movement of others much like a parent controls the actions of a child. They are often charismatic and manipulative. They feed off obedience and expect conformity (Gladding, 2001). Significant research has been conducted on the comparative impacts of democratic versus authoritarian leadership and democratic leaders do appear to be more successful in galvanizing group support and fostering positive group movement. However, effective leadership, much like effective membership, may be constituted mostly by these qualities and those components but never all of one and absolutely none of the other.

authority: The aspect of power in the group usually unconsciously assigned to the group leader but could be assigned to another group member. Group members vary in their reactions to perceived authority along a continuum of possibilities from submissive and dependent to rebellious and counterdependent. It is also possible to respond to authority with balance.

Black racial identity theories: Various theories that attempt to explain the various ways in which Blacks can identify (or not identify) with other Blacks and adopt or abandon identities resulting from racial victimization.

body language: The nonverbal messages most often conveyed unconsciously by an individual's physical reactions, expressions, body posture, facial expressions, and use of limbs. It is useful to be aware of one's own body language and to observe it in others.

boundaries: A concept borrowed from systemic thinking to denote psychological borders, limits, or encircling points of demarcation in groups and families. In counseling and therapy groups, members are encouraged to develop ground rules for working within the internal boundaries of the group rather than going into material and experiences beyond the external boundaries of the group.

catharsis: The release of pent-up or repressed emotions such as anger or joy that once expressed provide the group member relief. Catharsis is sometimes used as a synonym for *abreaction*, a psychoanalysis term for the therapeutic relieving of painful or distressing emotion by the client through calling into awareness experiences or material that has been repressed (Gladding, 2001).

climate: A concept that is similar to atmosphere that relates the feeling of the group environment in terms of its temperature or "weather."

collaboration: A cyclical process in which two or more persons within a group work toward a mutually agreed-upon objective. Collaboration may also refer to creative and egalitarian intergroups or interorganizational processes through which problems are solved or aspects of the culture are improved by personal and interpersonal learning, discovery, knowledge sharing, and the development of consensus.

congruence: The quality of matching or correspondence between one's speech and behavior in interpersonal interaction with others in the group. For example, a member who says, "I'm happy" but whose face has a scowling expression is said to lack congruence.

consensual validation: A term originated by Harry S. Sullivan (1953) that refers to the method by which interpersonal distortions are corrected. The method provides the member having a paratoxic (i.e., interpersonal) distortion an opportunity to correct the distortion by hearing the views of other group members with regard to an occasion in the group where such a distortion occurred (also discussed by Yalom, 1995).

content: The apparent topic or activity that usually occurs in the external dimension of group life and human interaction. It may be experienced audibly, visually, or both and may be perceived to be negative, positive, or indifferent.

corrective recapitulation of the primary family group: A term used by Yalom (1995) in reference to the possibility of altering "growth-inhibiting" (Yalom, p. 14) patterns of behavior learned in one's first and most important group experience, the family. Some of these inhibiting patterns may be due to unsatisfactory, sometimes even traumatic experiences in one's family. Thus, corrective recapitulation refers to the possibility that such experiences may be "relived correctively" in counseling and therapy groups.

counseling: The application of mental health, psychological or human development principles, through cognitive, affective, behavioral or systemic interventions, strategies that address wellness, personal growth, or career development, as well as pathology (American Counseling Association, 1997; Gladding, 2001).

curative factors: Eleven factors researched and described by Irvin Yalom (1995) that contribute to the betterment of individuals in a group. These 11 factors are instillation of hope, universality, imparting of information, altruism, corrective recapitulation of the primary family group, development of socialization techniques, imitative behavior, interpersonal learning, group cohesiveness, catharsis, and existential factors (Gladding, 2001).

democratic leader: A leader in a group who trusts others to develop their own potential and that of others. Such a leader serves as the facilitator and not as a director, thereby cooperating, collaborating, and sharing responsibilities (Gladding, 2001).

dependency: (a) A group member or person who presents himself/herself as helpless and incapable but refuses to accept constructive feedback or try new ways of behaving. Such persons are known as "help-rejecting complainers" who encourage the behavior of advice giving. (b) A descriptor of a relationship in which one person cannot or will not function without the aid or input of another (Gladding, 2001).

disclosure: The action by which a group member or members share, divulge, reveal, or make feelings, thoughts, reactions, and life experiences known to others in the group.

disturbing motive: From focal conflict theory. Refers to undisclosed secret wishes, private hopes, and personal concerns that members want to address in the group that compete with unexpressed fears about what will happen if they share them.

dyad: A one-to-one relationship between two people (Gladding, 2001). Dyads or "dyadic" activity sometimes relates to pairing subgroups that occur during group activities. But may also refer to one of several configurations (such as triads, quartets, or sextets) utilized by group leaders to facilitate learning or certain kinds of interpersonal communication activities within a larger group.

dynamic: A concept that refers primarily to psychological and emotional energy that affects motion within groups or change within a field of forces or a system, thus group dynamics. The term is also used as a noun to refer to certain kinds of energy between individuals or within a group; for example, a group-savvy person might refer to a conflictual, sexual, or hostile dynamic between certain members of the group.

empathize: To put oneself in another's place in regard to subjective perceptions and emotions and yet to keep one's objectivity. Empathizing requires a suspension of judgment and a response to another person that conveys sensitivity and understanding. It communicates understanding, fosters trust, and encourages deeper levels of the other's self-exploration (Gladding, 2001).

enabling solution: From focal conflict theory. Refers to a type of group solution whereby group members find a successful "solution" to an existing focal conflict. Enabling solutions are accepted by full-group consensus and help relieve anxiety related to reactive motives, which essentially are fears.

ethnicity: A group classification of individuals who share a unique social and cultural heritage, which includes customs, language, religion, etc., passed on from generation to generation (Casas, 1984).

experiential: This term often refers to an approach to group training and professional development in which participants learn by guided personal experience and interaction with other participants for educational or therapeutic purposes, in contrast to didactic models, which limit or eliminate the ongoing interactive component and rely more on formal and traditional academic learning modalities.

feedback: The sharing of perception of a behavior and relevant information with a group member so that the person can make decisions as to whether he or she would like to change. Feedback information should be given in a clear, concrete, succinct, and appropriate manner (Gladding, 2001). To this I would add that *appropriate* means that feedback should be based on the recipient's observable behavior, i.e., bodily action and speech. It is not appropriate, for example, to give feedback about a person's thinking or feelings per se. One can speculate about another person's thinking or feelings, but such speculation is out of the realm of constructive feedback unless the other guidelines are acknowledged and observed.

focal conflict: In focal conflict theory, a focal conflict results from competing, disturbing, and reactive motives.

group cohesiveness: The togetherness or closeness of a group, "we-ness." Cohesiveness in a group can be increased through friendly interaction, cooperation, increased group status, an outside threat, or democratic (as opposed to authoritarian) leadership (Gladding, 2001).

group collusion: Cooperating with others unconsciously or consciously to reinforce prevailing attitudes, values, behaviors, or norms. The purpose of such behavior is self-protection, and its effect is to maintain the status quo in the group (Gladding, 2001).

group counseling: Groups that focus on prevention, growth, and remedial issues that are both intrapersonal and interpersonal in nature. Sometimes these groups are known as *interpersonal problem-solving groups* (Gladding, 2001).

group culture: From focal conflict theory. Refers to a "composite of all prescriptions for group behavior which is similar to group normative structure. These prescriptions are established by the group's solutions to its various focal conflicts" (Kline, 2003, p. 76; Whitaker & Lieberman, 1964).

group dynamics: A term originally used by Kurt Lewin, a pioneer researcher and social science innovator who used the term originally to describe the interaction among members of a group (Gladding, 2001).

group solution: From focal conflict theory. Refers to the result and product of a group's effort to reduce anxiety and tension. A group solution is an acceptable answer to an existing focal conflict. The group solution may be either enabling or restrictive.

group therapy (also known as group psychotherapy): A group treatment that specializes in remediation or personality reconstruction. It is meant to help people who have serious psychological problems of a long-term duration. As such, this type of group is found most often in mental health facilities such as clinics and hospitals (Gladding, 2001).

homeostasis: The natural tendency of the group to seek a level of balance during its interaction and life as a group over time. It can be a problematic tendency within families, groups, and systems because it inclines toward remaining static and results in resisting change and keeping circumstances in a state of equilibrium (Gladding, 2001).

interpersonal: Between two or more group members (Gladding, 2001).

intervention: An action, initiative, or statement on the part of the group leader or therapist aimed at directing the group or certain members to notice the interaction they are engaged in and stop it or shift to something else.

intrapersonal: A synonym for *intrapsychic*; literally "within the person" (Gladding, 2001).

membership: The psychological state by which, according to the nature and quality of the relationship between the group and any one of its members, belongingness to the group is felt. Along a continuum with several permutations, the highest state of psychological membership exists when a member is highly attracted to the group and highly accepted by the group. Alternatively, the lowest psychological membership exists when a member has low attraction to the group and low acceptance by the group.

norms: Rules and standards of behavior that help the group more effectively maintain itself as a productive working unit if they are internalized by group members early on in the life of the group.

ownership: To take responsibility for what is your own thought, feeling, action or non-action, initiative or non-initiative, choosing or non-choosing as these impact yourself and/or others. "Taking ownership" also means to accept responsibility for any or all of these aspects of behavior. This acceptance of responsibility is usually demonstrated by the use of "I-language" rather than "You or We language." This requires that you express yourself in more personal, specific, and non-minimizing ways with regard to the above-mentioned aspects of behavior. For example, if someone hurts you, rather than saying "You feel kind of hurt when somebody does that to you." You would say "I feel really hurt when you do that to me."

parataxic distortion: A term from Sullivan (1953) that describes a process similar to transference but is more complex. According to Yalom (1995), it refers to a group member's tendency to "distort their perceptions of others" (p. 19). Further, Yalom says that such a distortion occurs in interpersonal interactions "when one person relates to another not on the basis of the realistic attributes of the other but on the basis of a personification existing chiefly in the former's own fantasy" (p. 19).

POC: People of Color.

process: The less apparent energy or feeling that accompanies content. It is the animating principle in group interaction. Matters relating to process are usually not audible or visible but are noticeable and clearly felt. When used as a verb in groups, process means to review or examine what has occurred during the course of interaction between members or within the group.

psychoeducational group: A group whose primary purpose is to educate or instruct its members in regard to certain subjects or areas pertinent to their lives (e.g., a parent education group; Gladding, 2001).

race: A subgroup of peoples possessing a definite combination of physical characters of genetic origin, the combination of which to varying degrees distinguishes the subgroup from other subgroups of mankind (Casas, 1984).

racial identity: A term that refers to an individual's sense of group or collective identity based on the perception that he or she shares a common racial heritage with a particular racial group.

racial identity development theory: Frameworks for understanding the psychological implications of racial group membership; that is, belief systems that evolve in reaction to perceived differential racial group membership (Helms, 1993).

reactive motive: From focal conflict theory. Refers to undisclosed or unexpressed fears anticipated to result from expression of the related disturbing motive in the group.

risk-taking: New behaviors that generate some anxiety but are taken by a group member in order to change behaviors and reach therapeutic goals (Gladding, 2001).

restrictive solution: From focal conflict theory. Refers to group solutions that may reduce fears associated with reactive motives but that do not satisfy the disturbing motive. Such solutions generally involve avoiding discussions related to the disturbing motive in the group.

self-awareness: An ongoing process in life of recognizing thoughts, emotions, senses, and behaviors that influence a person on multiple levels (Gladding, 2001). Shared experiences within the group, where members witness others grappling with challenges and issues of their lives, and also giving and receiving constructive feedback foster increased self-awareness.

solutional conflict: From focal conflict theory. Refers to an outcome that is the result of group members being unable to reach agreement on a solution to a particular focal conflict.

synergy: A cooperative interaction in which the energy or initiative of two or more individuals combines and works harmoniously to produce a positive result that exceeds what any single person could produce.

systems theory: A theoretical paradigm that includes a view of individuals, groups, and organizations as systems. Systems theory explains interactions within and between these larger and smaller parts of itself with regard to the regulation of member behavior, balance, commonalities, communication, and boundaries. Systems theory has been exceptionally useful to the field of small group studies, including group development theory and group counseling, group dynamics, family therapy, and also organization behavior and change.

themes: Recurring topics in the group that usually characterize issues that are not yet fully explored or certain emotion-laden challenges that hover in the group. In focal conflict theory, themes also represent the prevailing topic, overriding focus, common tension, or mutually shared concerns of the group.

therapy: A term sometimes used interchangeably with *psychotherapy* and *counseling*. Traditionally, therapy and psychotherapy have been used to describe psychological interventions with clients who have serious (as opposed to mild) disturbances and disorders. Therapy and psychotherapy are also traditionally associated with long-term treatment, although this distinction has become blurred in recent years with the onset of brief therapy (Gladding, 2001).

VREG: Visible racial ethnic group.

White racial identity theories: Theories that attempt to explain the various ways in which Whites can identity (or not identify) with other Whites and/or evolve or avoid evolving a nonoppressive White identity (Helms, 1993).

work: Activities that are engaged in for gain or reward rather than for pleasure that might be derived from them (Gladding, 2001). Within the group context, a member or group collective is said to be doing the work when his, her, or their effort and initiatives are consistently unconflicted, fostering increased self-awareness, or facilitating positive group movement.

worldview: An individual's perception of the world based on his or her experiences, as well as the socialization processes of the person in interaction with members of his or her reference group (i.e., culture, country, social, or ethnic community). Worldviews directly affect and mediate people's belief systems, assumptions, models of problem solving, decision making, and conflict resolution styles. The four most prevalent worldviews as proposed by Sue (1978) are internal locus of control and responsibility, external locus of control and responsibility, external locus of control/internal locus of responsibility, and internal locus of control/external locus of responsibility (Gladding, 2001).

Group Stages Introduction

This section introduces the group stage Chapters, 1 through 4, which are presented after this discussion. The introduction includes a preliminary review of group development stage models, a discussion of key aspects of multicultural and diversity awareness in groups, and finally an explanation of the scenarios that are included in group stage chapter discussion.

Although critically important events such as the establishment of norms for productive interaction and participation should be launched in the beginning stages of counseling, experiential, and therapy groups, it has been my personal experience that the most productive and growth-facilitating activity frequently occurs in the middle stages of the group. The least productive activity most often occurs in the ending or terminating group stages (Garland, Jones, & Kilodny, 1965; Tuckman, 1965; Wheelan, Tsumura, & Kline, 1998). For this reason and for simplicity, I have organized my discussion of group development stages into four parts. These include beginning, early middle, late middle, and terminating stages. I have designated a chapter for each of these stages, with a discussion that includes the characteristics of the stage, major group challenges, and major member challenges of the stage, each from the point of view of things that may be helpful for you as a member to notice. Scenarios that follow each chapter's discussion are further discussed later.

Most stage models are variations of a simple three-part concept, namely, beginning, middle, and end or initial, working, and terminating stages. In my approach to organization, I have divided the middle stage into two parts, representing the early and late stages of work. Though I did not set out with the objective of presenting a new theory of group development, I recognize that my reordering of currently existing stage models actually does create another model of group stages. Nonetheless, my primary aim has only been to arrange the book this way for simplicity and ease of presentation. Group theorists have established more complex group stage development models. However, I have arranged discussion of their developmental and interpersonal group theories within the context of my own stages. However, I have attempted to place more attention on the challenges of becoming an effective group member than on the challenges of effective group leadership.

I think it is useful to understand that all newly formed groups move through observable stages of development and change. Descriptions set forth by group theorists vary in terms of how simple or complex stages or phases are. Themes related to these stages usually address attempts by group members to handle anxiety associated with keeping balance in the group and maintaining growth-enhancing interpersonal boundaries. Each stage of a group may also consist of an indeterminate number of "cycles" that circle progressively forward, counter-progressively backwards, or which hover in what appears to be suspended animation or "stuckness."

Most group theorists (Bennis & Shepard, 1956, 1970; Bion, 1961; Corey, M.S. & Corey, G., 2006; Donigian & Malnati, 1997; Kline, 2003; Schutz, 1966) identify recognizable interpersonal issues and challenges for each stage. Yalom (1995) cautions that even though he has outlined stages in his text, they are not to be taken too literally because the phases or stages only represent constructs that are created by leaders for their own conceptual convenience. Yalom also states that there is no empirical proof that group stages "do or must exist" in the therapeutic process. Further, he observes that "boundaries between phases are not clearly demarcated, nor does a group permanently graduate from one phase" (p. 303).

MULTICULTURAL AND DIVERSITY AWARENESS

I have included an introductory discussion of multicultural diversity and awareness because of its looming importance at this time. It is not my aim to present a comprehensive multicultural handbook for group members. Rather, it is my intention to acknowledge the relevance of the issue from the perspective of self-awareness. Hill (2003) observes how it has become increasingly evident that we in the United States are a multicultural, multiethnic, and multilingual society (p. 39). Further, she cites Holcomb-McCoy and Myers (1999), Ochs (1994), U.S. Bureau of the Census (1992), and Whitfield (1994) in substantiation of her observation.

Certainly, the global impact of the election of the first African American president of the United States has become increasingly apparent. Moreover, the U.S. demographic reality is undergoing extraordinary change due to the explosive growth of its Hispanic population. This change, when considered together with the impact of other minority groups, including African Americans, Asians, and Native Americans, is shifting non-Whites toward becoming 50% of the population.

Such changes in the cultural composition of America not only affect you in present groups to which you belong or in which you participate for academic or therapeutic reasons. These changes also affect individuals, neighborhoods, and communities in social sciences and the helping professions, as well as in medicine, science, education, business, law, and others.

Multicultural and diversity issues include ethnic and racial changes in the society, cultural, and cross-cultural concerns as relate to one's worldview, and to the collective historical experience of the society's peoples. The executive board of the Association for Specialists in Group Work (ASGW, 1998) took a broad perspective in its view of the multicultural phenomenon. The board agreed that diversity competence for group workers should mean demonstrated "comfort, tolerance, and sensitivity with differences that exist between themselves and group members in terms of race, ethnicity, culture, socioeconomic status (SES), gender, sexual orientation, abilities, religion, and spirituality and their beliefs, values, and biases" (p. 2). Likewise, this perspective should mean that you as an effective group member strive to achieve a fundamental level of insightful multicultural awareness such as may lead you to increased diversity competence according to your degree of interest in its pursuit and establishment in your life.

WORLDVIEW

Worldview is the overall perspective from which an individual or group sees and understands the world. It includes personal and collective "views" and beliefs about oneself and other human beings, as well as about life and the universe. For some, worldview is a model of reality that describes how things are in terms of social affairs, values, and one's way of thinking about one's utmost priorities, whatever they are.

Worldview concerns and issues involve questions of racism and disparate treatment of minority persons. Attempts to justify such behavior most often include rationalized prejudice based upon one or more disqualifiers. These include "faulty" ethnicity, gender, socioeconomic status, religious, sexual orientation, or other egocentric "I–Thou" frames of reference that make one self-selected category of humans superior to others.

Included are perceptions of a person's relationship to the world as well as assumptions about human nature, social relationships, the natural world, time, and activity that directly affect one's problem-solving style, thinking, and decision-making processes. Some counselors also hold the view that the way one perceives the world affects one's perceptions of others. With regard to worldview, the challenges are mainly two. The first is to avoid stereotyping and judging others. The second is to avoid insisting that the "reality" or "truth" of what exists can only be as you see it through your own personal lens onto the world.

MULTICULTURAL DEVELOPMENT IN GROUPS

Multicultural groups follow general stage models as discussed earlier. Members face characteristically identifiable interpersonal issues and challenges. The exception is that in a dedicated multicultural group, leader initiatives may more actively explore the extent to which self-knowledge, particularly with regard to "insightful awareness" of how one relates to diverse others, is affected by the racial, ethnic, and cultural context into which one is born and lives. The objective or hope is that as one's self-knowledge increases, respect for others and acceptance of their differences will also increase.

BOWMAN'S MODEL OF SELF-AWARENESS FOR MULTICULTURAL TRAINING

Bowman's (1996) model is particularly useful because of its view of the role of self-awareness in multicultural competence. The components of the model are (a) learning about oneself; (b) learning about others; and (c) learning about how one relates to others. Because of the emphasis placed on self-awareness and self-exploration in the prologue and stage chapters of this text, some basis has already been established by which you can extend your awareness and your knowledge and skill into the area of multicultural competence in groups.

Learning About Self

In this component, Bowman (1996) affirms the importance of self-knowledge as a prerequisite to working with others. She encourages a "sensitization process" for learners who are White and for learners who are People of Color. Bowman also suggests that an initial focus on White culture is appropriate because minority groups are often underrepresented in training programs. Additionally, researchers have suggested that what is missing for White trainees is self-exploration as members of the White race (Corvin & Wiggins, 1989). Katz (1978) notes that "Whites don't see themselves as White," (p. 13) further pointing out that Whites most often incline to their ethnic heritage as a means of self-identification rather than toward their racial origins or background.

Bowman (1996) presents ideas for several configurations of groups in which issues of privilege, power, prejudice, racism, identity, race, and culture may be explored. Included are groups composed solely of non-Whites, Whites or groups consisting of non-Whites and Whites together. Bowman also gives suggestions for group member safety in terms of providing an environment where there is time, opportunity, and support for examining concerns that may spark feelings of defensiveness and guilt before participants reach stages of insight, autonomy, and internalization.

Learning About Others

Bowman (1996) mentions that information on various ethnic and racial groups is voluminous and that when the exploration is extended to other diverse populations such as relate to gender, including gay, lesbian, bisexual, transgendered, and abilities concerns, the scope is so significantly broadened that only superficial attention can be given to any topic. Bowman therefore suggests supplemental use of literature and media resources but also gives cautions regarding stereotypes, as well as unrealistic learner expectations, as these contrast with the scope of culturally related material that exists (see Appendix B).

Learning About How One Relates to Others

Here Bowman (1996) discusses the importance of experiential training and direct contact with culturally different peoples in order to move from one who knows that cultural differences exist to one who knows how to interact effectively and with self-confidence in relationship to persons who are culturally different from oneself.

REGARDING GROUP SCENARIOS

As you likely know by now, each chapter's group stage discussion is supported by related scenarios that exemplify challenges of the stage for the group, as well as for its members and for you. The purpose of the scenarios is to illustrate potential challenges for the group as a whole and for you as a member during the particular stage addressed by each chapter. My aim is to provide you with experiential examples of what group interaction and intermember behavior might actually look like within various group stages. The scenarios present the group and its members in such a way as to enable you to gain insight into various member personalities, as well as into members' family and cultural backgrounds that influence interpersonal relationships and dynamics of the group. Alternate endings to the scenarios are presented for the purpose of showing different possible directions that group interactions may take.

Also, please note that as the reader, you will be incorporated into the scenarios throughout the text. In most instances, you will be addressed simply as "you." In circumstances where there is a need to refer to you objectively, your name will always be "Youtu." Because you are projected into the story of each scenario as a participant, possibilities are extended to you whereby you may further expand your knowledge, awareness, insight, and experiential understanding of how one becomes a facilitative and effective member of a counseling or therapy group. Each chapter's group stage discussion and presentation of scenarios is followed by a brief review of multicultural considerations for the scenarios. The aim here is to begin to glimpse the group from the perspective of multicultural and diversity awareness for the possibility of insights that may be gained. Finally, each stage chapter closes with questions for chapter review followed by selected prologue tips that are relevant for the particular group stage that is under discussion.

1

Beginning Stage

MAJOR MEMBER CHALLENGES IN THE BEGINNING STAGE

Several group theorists cite anxiety as one of the most prevalent emotional features of beginning groups (Bennis & Shepard, 1956, 1970; Bion, 1961; Corey, M.S. & Corey, G., 2006; Donigian & Malnati, 1997; Kline, 2003; Schutz, 1966; Yalom, 1995). This anxiety usually stems from the sense of ambiguity and uncertainty that members are likely to feel as they attempt to understand what to do in the unfamiliar social setting of the group. As a new member, you may notice that in the beginning stages of group life, you will face two types of challenges: The first involves learning how to deal with ambiguity and anxiety. The second involves discovering how to make meaningful initiatives within the new group setting where clear guidelines for what is productive behavior within the group may appear to be lacking.

CHARACTERISTICS OF THE BEGINNING STAGE: HELPFUL THINGS TO NOTICE

If you find that there is something anxiety provoking and ambiguous in the atmosphere of a new group, consider it as normal. Depending on the group leader's style, it may seem to you and to others in the group that a clearly stated goal is lacking. You may notice that members are sometimes hesitant to step forward to say what their feelings are as they wait for the leader to show them what to do or for someone else to step up. On the other hand, you may possibly find that an assertive new group member will attempt to fill the gap by suggesting ways group members can introduce themselves to each other or do activities that add structure and direction by asking things like, "Where are you from? What degree do you hold or are you pursing? What group courses or experiences with therapy have you had in the past?" You may notice that some members repeatedly look to the leader to make something happen. You can begin your work to become an effective group member by taking good notice of the group atmosphere and noticing your reactions as you are coming into the group. You can look around to see what other members do and you can listen carefully to what they say. You can also notice periods of silence that occur among members who seem engaged but not actively talking. You can also notice body movement and nonverbal interaction and behavior, commonly known as *body language*. You will always be encouraged to observe yourself in the group. It will always be helpful to think of how you are feeling and to notice what your own thoughts are now that you are here in the group. Taking the initiative to say what you notice in your own thoughts and feelings or sharing things about your reactions to others in an honest but noncritical way can be a particularly effective thing to do at this time and possibly at other times yet to come.

BEGINNING STAGE GROUP CHALLENGES: GOOD THINGS FOR YOU AS A MEMBER TO NOTICE

As the group works to ward off anxiety borne of apparent lack of structure and direction as to exactly what to do, it will be useful for you to notice what methods you and fellow group members may use to address the possible challenge of not feeling a part of the new and unusual social environment of the group. By *methods* I mean member tendencies toward participating in an active and engaged way versus actively withdrawing and resisting possible engagement and involvement. When group members attempt to avoid anxiety by repeatedly looking to the leader to tell them what to do, by looking to some impressive member, or even by looking to some counterdependent rebellious-seeming member who seems to need no one, it will be very helpful for you to listen to and notice what members say and do. You will then be able to choose to interact or not by sharing what you hear and notice. If you have the view that what is happening is not facilitative or helpful, you may request that the member or the group consider trying an alternative tact. You might even attempt to share your feelings or encourage another member to share his or her feelings in the face of the anxiety, apparent lack of structure, lack of help from the leader, or unexpressed hopes for what he or she wants or hopes to accomplish by attending the group.

Reflecting on How You Deal With Authority (or Power) and Closeness

Taking time to engage in some honest reflection and introspection about your orientation to authority and closeness in relationship to others can be helpful. This may include reflecting on your experiences in your family or beliefs that you hold based on the culture you feel yourself to be a part of or other social, religious, or ethnic mores you or your family members live by. I encourage you to learn from the interactions, struggles, resistances, and risks that others show through their behavior in the group. Give yourself permission to say aloud what you notice about yourself, about your own thoughts, questions, hesitancy, as well as what you notice about other group members including the leader or therapist. Try out things you might not ordinarily try. See what happens. It may also be helpful to know that a key responsibility of the group leader in the beginning stage deals with helping the group establish norms or basic rules for working in the here and now, even while group members may be grappling with other issues having to do with ambiguity and group structure. Taking it as your responsibility to understand the skill of here and now awareness and utilizing it in context can be highly facilitative and important. It is also important to recognize when you and other members do not observe this simple guideline. Notice when you or other members slip into or actively choose to engage in insubstantial chatting, highly general or outside topics of discussion, in an attempt to fill the space or ward off vague, uneasy feelings that may come up in yourself or in the group.

BEGINNING STAGE MEMBER CHALLENGES: MORE GOOD THINGS FOR YOU TO NOTICE

Implications for you as a member in terms of the challenges of this stage largely involve acquiring, accessing, and utilizing the following things throughout group sessions:

1. Self-awareness
2. Alert observation
3. Initiating skills

After this, you must understand the critical importance of here and now discussion and management of external boundaries of the group. These two things are helpful in keeping group time and interpersonal exchanges increasingly more focused on interactions within the life of the group that are shared by all members who are present.

In my view, part of the development of productive here and now norms means that a ground rule develops among members that if a member must resort to history or experiences outside those of the group, he or she must take the responsibility to say what has happened here (in this group) that makes entering the discussion important. That member must also show how the discussion relates to what is happening with him- or herself in the here and now of this group. This means that each member shares the responsibility for not presenting topics that, if entered into, distract the group from its more important work. Usually, unless someone notices and intervenes, the result of such distractions is that members continue to pursue them until finally the group is adrift, as if it were a life boat lost at sea. Once you have understood the challenges for the group and for yourself during this stage, then you bear the responsibility to notice what you think, say, and do as well as the extent to which your behavior meets the norm in a facilitative way. After noticing yourself comes the challenge of noticing the behavior of others, which means to notice what other members say and do. And finally, to take personal action by making initiatives to share or say what you notice about yourself in terms of your own thoughts and feelings, then to make initiatives to say what you notice, think of, feel, or react to from others throughout the course of group interaction.

BEGINNING STAGE SCENARIOS

Beginning Stage Characteristics: Scenario 1

Doreen, a 21-year-old art major in her senior year, and Bill, a 22-year-old junior majoring in biology, attend the same college as you. You have seen them around the campus but never spent time in the same social circles. Recently, you signed up for a counseling group offered by the campus counseling center. You attend a prescreening for the workshop where you share with Rick, the group facilitator, that you are a graduate student in counselor education. You want to participate in the workshop because you are emotionally exhausted as a result of having been thrown into a mediator role by parents who have recently decided to divorce and who incidentally are from different ethnic backgrounds. Rick, who is 29, shares with you that he is now at the dissertation stage and working to complete his PhD in counseling psychology. You feel positively about the pregroup interview and Rick suggests that you will have a lot to offer and much to gain from the group. When you enter the room where the group convenes, you find that the atmosphere is pleasant and there are nine very comfortable chairs arranged in a circle. Even though you are on time, you are the last group member to arrive. You feel slightly relieved to see Doreen and Bill in the group. Doreen smiles at you, and Bill just glances over his glasses with indifference. One or two of the strangers say "Hi" and Rick welcomes you in a friendly way. He addresses you by name and says, "I'm glad you could come." Rick introduces himself to the group and talks about his graduate studies and his interest in the counseling field. He also explains the purpose of the group as personal growth, increased self-awareness, and improved effectiveness in relationships with others. The group will achieve these aims, in part, by members sharing their experiences, whether broad or limited, toward these ends. Rick also says that other objectives are to learn about the experiences of others and forge new interpersonal connections. He mentions understanding how in spite of the fact that several of the people present attended the pregroup interview, it is understandable that some persons still may have come into the group with a sense of hesitancy and feelings of uneasiness, not knowing what to expect. Then he says, in an easy-going, natural way that reminds you of how comfortable he made you feel at the pregroup interview, "How about if we just start by introducing ourselves. If you want to add anything about what made you decide to come to this group, feel free to share that too. I've already shared a little about me, so I'm just going to turn it over to the group. We don't have to follow any special order. Just speak up when you're ready, okay?"

A full 60 seconds of silence follow Rick's comments. The 60 seconds feel like 60 minutes. Bill slides down in his seat. He alternates between looking toward the window and checking the markings on his sneakers. Doreen glances at you now and then but she seems to hang on Rick's every word. Finally, one or two people venture forth. Their names are José and Julie, who says she goes by what sounds to you like "Jewels." José, a 22-year-old senior, says that he is a psychology major interested in all kinds of people. One of his parents is from Oaxaca, Mexico. Jewels, a 20-year-old sophomore, then says that she is a theater major and that one of the communications courses for her program requires a group experience. During the introductions, Doreen continues to glance at Rick intermittently. You wonder if she likes the group leader or if she wants him to notice her. You wonder if she wants to leave the room or what. You wonder why she does not speak up. You notice that you have many private thoughts about her but you do not say anything to her, even though you want to. In your mind, you also review your own reasons for having come to the group. You rehearse what you might say "if push comes to shove" but you do not come forward on your own to share a single thing. You still have thoughts about that long silence after Rick's introduction. You are wondering what is happening with Bill, who seems very bored to you. At last, Rick notices Doreen's glance. She averts her eyes but she begins to speak. "Hi," she says as she looks nervously at the floor. "I'm Doreen. I'm here because I am an only child … at least I thought I was. Recently, I discovered that I have a 12-year-old brother. We have the same dad but my brother's mother is Black."

Beginning Stage Group Challenges: Scenario 2

When members meet for the second session, there is yet a bit of lingering anxiety and hesitancy in the group. This anxiety mixes with a feeling of mild anticipation that members still feel in the atmosphere. Doreen's disclosure about the discovery of a brother born of her father's relationship with an African American woman happened in the final minutes of the group's first session. Rick, the leader, had acknowledged Doreen's comments before the group concluded. "It appears to me," he said, "that your discovery about your father's relationship with another woman who bore him a son, whom you're now discovering twelve years or more after the fact, is something that is having quite an impact on you right now." The force of Doreen's disclosure seemed to have completely drained her body of its energy. Her ruddy complexion faded to gray. She answered Rick with a sigh that seemed to rise up to her chest from the tips of her toes. "Yea-aaah," she said. "I wish I had the words the first time I heard it to say how much it affected me. This discovery has definitely rocked my world. I feel like I've been blessed and cursed at the same time."

"I'm very thankful for what you've shared with us," Rick said. "I hope that we can make this group a place where you and others can share your feelings and concerns. However, right now, we're at the end of our time for this session. I want to thank you all for being here. I look forward to seeing everybody next time."

At the beginning of Session 2 today, Rick welcomes the members again. After everyone is settled Rick says, "Hello, everybody. It's good to see you back. How are you all doing today?" Doreen says, "Fine." Bill nods and José says, "Good." Jewels gives a thumbs up and two of the three remaining silent members show their first signs of life. Maria, a 23-year-old sophomore social work major, who refers to herself as Ria, gives a shy hello, then smiles and says, "I'm good." Then a young woman, Chris, a 26-year-old music major and undisclosed recovering alcoholic says, "Hi." Finally, Tony, a 35-year-old Vietnamese American mature adult student in his junior year, squirms around in his seat and says, "I'm sorta doing okay but I just want to ask why do people have to go through so much pain? This planet that we live on is nothing but a freakin' *Titanic*. Know what I mean?" No one, including you, really understands exactly what is behind the words and their glaring cynicism. You wonder but you don't risk asking. When you finally are about to tell Tony that you wonder about what he said, Bill sits up in his chair and beats you to the punch. "I can relate to what you say, man, about people going through pain," he says. "It's obvious that the world is like you said, 'a freakin' mess.'" Rick's eyebrows shoot up like window shades. He appears interested in the activity that is happening. He looks at Tony and Bill and then he looks around the group. He also looks at you but he only smiles for a moment and continues looking at the others. All eyes are upon Tony and Bill. When Tony realizes that everyone is looking at him, he sits forward in his chair and stares at the floor as if he is looking over the edge of a cliff. When his hands begin to shake almost involuntarily, he stands up and says, "I gotta go. I mean it was nice to meet you all, but I'm all messed up. I've got to leave."

Rick immediately speaks up.

> You're absolutely free to go if you have to, Tony, but I wish you'd stick around. It sounds like there are things happening now or that have happened before that are really on your mind in here. You'd being doing us all a big favor if you stuck around. Man, I see your hands shaking and what you said was kind of cryptic, but it sure hit me with power and it probably hit others in here, too. I wonder if you'd be willing to put off leaving and hang in here with us for at least another session. It would be great if you would share a bit of what happened here that led you to say the things you did. I wonder if you'd be willing to hear more from Bill and others who seem to be affected by what you said.

Tony's face seems to fill up with anguish but he doesn't turn around and leave the room. He just nods as Rick asks questions, then he sits back down in his chair. Rick looks around the group and waits for the group to make its next steps.

Beginning Stage Member Challenges: Scenario 3

Another long silence in the group follows Rick's remarks to Tony. Something in his words and way of reaching out to Tony catches everyone's attention. Bill's response to Tony's disclosure and his threat to leave the group, followed by Rick's attempt to slow down the action and gain a better understanding of Tony's pain, seem to electrify the group. No one speaks up after Rick's remarks, but it is apparent that everyone has listened. Every group member's eyes continue to be pinned on Tony, with occasional glances to Rick as if they hoped he might say more to Tony. You have wanted to say many things since the first group meeting, and you wanted to say something to Tony, but Bill responded before you did. Rick's last words before the group silence are still ringing in your ears because he has left an opening for you and any other group member by telling Tony it seemed that Bill as well as others who had not yet spoken were affected by Tony's words and behavior. You notice your own thoughts; you notice that something in yourself was touched by Tony's words. You also notice a hint of feeling like a failure when Bill speaks up before you but you remain frozen nonetheless. You have made some attempts to analyze your stuckness, but for the most part, your thoughts have only gone around in a circle. After you follow your thoughts for another moment or two, you notice that the room is too warm. Your collar is too tight and your mouth is dry. You move your lips but no words come out. Rick notices you with a sympathetic glance but he doesn't say anything to help. You notice beads of perspiration forming on your forehead and it feels like the temperature in the room is rising. As you glance at the two closed windows just across the room from you, the thought comes to ask Rick if they can be opened, but his attention seems to be elsewhere. Suddenly, with no preparation, words that are even surprising to you fly out of your mouth: "Can … can … can somebody tell me what the heck we're doing here?" you say. Rick responds to you by saying, "I wonder if you might be trying to tell us that you feel lost because you think the group has no purpose. Or maybe you're feeling nervous and anxious about telling me or the group that you want someone to tell you and other members what the heck to do?"

Before you can say a word, in answer to Rick, Bill responds to the question saying, "I don't need nobody to tell me what to do. I can take care of myself just fine." Bill seems to have directed his words to you and his tone is angry. A familiar feeling you felt in your family as a child flashes up in you, like when your father blamed you for something that was your sibling's fault. Surprisingly, words fly out of your mouth again when you look at Bill and say, "Maybe you really believe that you don't need anybody to tell you what to do, but I think the words you just said need to be directed to Rick and not to me." Bill's pause and shocked expression give you a bit of satisfaction. You have a sense of having done the right thing for yourself regardless of whether he likes it or not. You notice that you are no longer perspiring and your mouth is not so dry anymore.

Beginning Stage Scenario 3: Alternative Ending A

Before Bill can respond, Chris speaks up and says, "I'm really embarrassed to bring this up but I always have problems remembering names … and I really want to remember here. Could we take a minute to hear people's names again and maybe even say where you're from. As you know, I'm Chris. My major is music and I'm originally from Nevada, actually from Spring Valley, which is not too far from Las Vegas." Bill gives Chris a harsh look but some of the other members seem relieved. Until you blurted out your question about what people are supposed to be doing in the group, nothing much seemed to be happening except a lot of silence. Group members seemed to pay attention when Tony stood up and threatened to leave the group, but neither you nor anyone else except Rick, the leader, has managed to really step up to make a meaningful initiative. You have noticed many things in the group, you have noticed yourself having reactions, but until now you've been silent and if you were honest about how other group members see you right now, you'd guess they were describing you as someone who is lost in her or his own thoughts. Your musings are interrupted by Jewels, who mentions how nice the weather has been. "Sunny days always lift my spirits," she says. "I was really happy walking here today." One or two group members echo feelings of being uplifted by sunshine too. When José introduces himself, he tells that his surname is Banderas and Chris asks if he is related to the film star, Antonio Banderas. Rick looks on all the while but the members seem to ignore him. The group atmosphere becomes light, almost like a bottle of champagne was just popped. The group descends into a round of heady chatter about upcoming movies and half the members are participating. The only ones on the fringes of this discussion are Doreen, Bill, Tony, you, and Rick. Finally, Rick speaks up and says, "I'm very happy to see folks trying to get things going in our group, but I wonder if group members notice what's gone on in the last ten or fifteen minutes. Perhaps it feels very nice, but really it's missing the target in terms of what actually needs to happen here." Group members appear to be stunned by Rick's comments.

Beginning Stage Scenario 3: Alternative Ending B

Again, before Bill reacts, Doreen speaks up and says, "I'm feeling like we all have dropped Tony. I'm really hoping he'll stick around. I wonder how other people here feel." Rick looks around the group in his usual interested way. Bill looks back at him but he does not pick up on your challenge to readdress his words to the leader. Meanwhile several members, including José, Jewels, Chris, and Maria, respond to Doreen's initiative and make attempts to express their interest in Tony. In spite of her shy persona, Maria is one of the most expressive group members, who conveys unexpected, touching empathy for Tony. "I don't know what your pain is, but I feel it. I'm sorry you see the planet like a sinking ship. I hope you don't drown. I don't really know you very well at all, but something about you makes me feel like you really are a good guy. I hope you stick around so I can see if you really are or not." After observing this exchange, it seems to you that Bill is affected by Maria's outpouring of concern to Tony. In fact, you think that Bill might even wish that Maria was saying her words to him. You don't mention this, though. You recognize that Bill irks you, so if you say anything in this moment, rather than expressing your honest reactions to Tony, Maria, and other members of the group, you'd just be trying to mete out some payback for his harshness towards you. Rick has the final words before the session approaches its end. "I feel hopeful for our group," he says. "Many good things happened here today. Rather than me going through them now, maybe sometime in the future we can hear your ideas about what's going well or what's missing in our group from your points of view."

Multicultural Considerations: Beginning Stage

Already we can see that this group is multicultural and diverse in its composition, even though it is not primarily designated as a multicultural group. The group has eight members and includes two biracial men, three White women, one African American woman, one Mexican American man, and a member (Youtu) who is of unknown gender and ethnic origin. The group leader is an African American man. The consideration that any group might already be multicultural or more diverse than one realizes is significant. In some way, our journey to true diversity awareness begins as soon as we recognize that we have no idea who others are as judged solely by their appearance. Add to this complex member experiences related to their genders, family histories, and emotional lives. Such "chunk of life" aspects as these make it very clear that the multicultural and diversity awareness landscape to be charted in both the group and the world classroom is vast.

In the first scenario, Beginning Stage: Scenario 1, Doreen, a 21-year-old White woman discloses her recent discovery that she has a 12-year-old half brother fathered by her father and another woman. We also see the apparent ethnic diversity of the members as discussed previously. In Scenario 2, Rick, the group leader, picks up on Doreen's disclosure, which came in the closing moments of the first group session. It is interesting that no one, including Rick, comments on Doreen's remark about how she felt herself to be affected by the discovery of her father having a 12-year-old son whose mother is Black. Doreen had said, "This discovery has definitely rocked my world. I feel like I've been blessed and cursed at the same time." Such a comment could be viewed as anything ranging from innocence to provocative to inflammatory. In a group with as much diversity as the one in which Doreen is a member, it is highly likely that some member would in the least acknowledge the remark and, ideally, ask to hear more from Doreen about her meaning and what she is trying to say. More of the group's diversity is revealed as we learn about Tony's biracial ethnic origins, that he is a Vietnamese American man. Ria, the African American young woman, and two White young women, Jewels and Chris, also take some small steps toward making their presence felt in the group. Tony's disclosure that "This planet that we live on is nothing but a freakin' *Titanic*" has apparent impact on the group. Because it has no context, members have no clue as to whether it has underlying racial or ethnic tension or not, so it presents a challenge and discovery to be made. In the third scenario, the leader's response to Tony has an impact on the group. Bill somehow becomes connected to Tony in his response to Tony's remark, and in the end, Youtu, who has been relatively quiet, finally makes an entrée into the group. In Alternative Ending A, Chris and José venture into the group activity, but the group members are engaged in small talk and no real work is done until Rick intervenes with the group. Finally, in Alternative Ending B, Doreen speaks up on behalf of Tony, whom she believes has been left out by the group. It is an interesting interaction and one cannot help but wonder if there are unspoken dynamics at work because of the impact of her having discovered that she has a 12-year-old brother who is biracial. Maria expresses powerful empathy for Tony's pain, which seems to affect Bill. His facial expressions suggest that he is affected but he does not say any words that give any definitive idea of what he might be feeling. Having observed these interactions and reviewed the scenarios, how would you answer the following questions?

QUESTIONS FOR CHAPTER REVIEW

1. What do you notice about the group leader? Was his intervention with Tony facilitative? Do you think that he is a good model of what a leader should be?
2. How would you describe yourself as a member in this group? What must you do more or less of in order to become an effective member in the scenario group?

3. If this group was a dedicated multicultural awareness group and you were asked to introduce yourself according to your ethnic identification or cultural background, what would you say?
4. In thinking back on the group scenarios from the perspective of Bowman's model of self-awareness, what aspect of the developments has the greatest possibility of leading you to any important learning or discovery about yourself, about others, or about how you relate to others?
5. What lessons can you take from the scenarios that might help you to be more personally effective as a member of the group?

PART 1 PROLOGUE TIPS FOR THE BEGINNING STAGE

Key Components of an Effective Member Mindset

Understand the Purpose of the Group

- Ask yourself: What you expect to be the purpose of the group you are about to enter?
- If this group experience is your first, or one of few you may have had, it is possible that you are entering with some uncertainty about what will happen.
- Are you willing to begin this self-discovery process?
- Entering a group for personal growth or other reasons can sometimes create anxiety, especially if it feels like you are entering unknown territory and you don't know what to expect. Understand that this is normal.
- If your group has members from diverse ethnic, racial, or cultural backgrounds, understand that discussion and interaction around issues related to these aspects can be highly emotionally charged.
- If you have had other experiences, you may be coming with impressions based on how things were for you at that time.
- During the process of interaction, you will have opportunities to gain counseling, self-awareness, and interpersonal communications skills, through the activities of the group.
- You will have many opportunities to discover things about yourself in terms of what your strengths are in your relations with others and what the impacts of your particular style of communication are.
- You will have a chance to acquire strategies for dealing with conflict in your life, for being more productive in situations of conflict, and for fostering growth and positive change in others.

Check Your Attitude

- Understand that your personal reactions and feelings can be your keys to effectiveness.
- After noticing, when you are ready, share your thoughts and say what you feel in the group.

- (Understand that) a member with a facilitative attitude is open to listening, sharing thoughts and feelings, and relating to the experiences of others.
- (Understand that) a member with a nonfacilitative attitude is closed off by choice.
- Mainly: Remain self-aware and share your reactions. Interpersonal connection and involvement is essential to your positive progress in the group.

Open Yourself to Discovery

- It can be surprising and challenging to face the expectation to be open in a group because it goes against many prevalent societal norms that support being superficial.
- The cultivation of openness among members of a group can greatly help in developing trust and reducing defensiveness.
- Mainly: Constructive openness involves risk and benefit. You are continuously choosing and taking chances, one moment at a time.

Understand that Experiential Learning May Be Different From What You Ordinarily Expect

- Often people who are new to experiential group settings find that what is to be learned sometimes is not clear.
- In experiential groups you have multiple teachers. Each member has at least one thing to offer that you do not have, which is his or her perception and experience of you.
- It behooves you to actually seek to discover what reactions and feelings other members hold about how and who you are.
- Mainly: Closing yourself off in moments of ambiguity may close you off from an opportunity to discover or learn.
- Hulse-Killacky, Killacky and Donigian's (2001) three questions are good to keep in mind in the group: Who am I? Who am I with? Who are we together?
- Open and honest communication and exchange between members is the sign of effective interaction.

Understand That Not Having Perfect Clarity and Being Uncomfortable Are Okay

- Maintaining inner balance during moments of uncertainty or when clear direction is lacking is another key to effective participation in groups.
- In the group, it is more helpful to think that you must take chances in order to be comfortable rather than think that you must be comfortable to take chances (J. Eveland, personal communication, April 2002).

- A key to effective membership and group participation is that you remain alert in the face of disempowering fear that may arise from uncertainty and discomfort.
- Rogers (1969) says it well: "All significant learning is to some degree painful and involves turbulence, within the individual and within the system" (p. 157).

Keep in Mind the Interactive Processes of Group Work

- The central focus of group work is interpersonal.
- Every counseling and therapy group is a three-element system.
- Open and honest communication and exchange between members is the sign of effective interaction.
- Group development is tied to key interpersonal issues which are involvement, dependency, authenticity, individuation, intimacy, and loss and loneliness (Kline, 2003).
- Hulse-Killacky, Killacky and Donigian's (2001) three questions are good to keep in mind in the group: Who am I? Who am I with you? Who are we together?

Learn How to Think in Process Terms and Distinguish Between Content and Process

- Your answer to the question, "What is happening in the group?" will likely identify something related to content.
- Your answer to the questions "How are things happening in this group?" and "What is the feeling/tone that accompanies 'the what'?" will likely identify something related to process.

Choose to Become a Group-Work Apprentice

- Any apprentice seeking mastery must qualify by three steps upon entering her or his apprenticeship. Namely, these are interest, openness to discovery, and willingness to change.

PART 2 PROLOGUE TIPS FOR THE BEGINNING STAGE

Basic Strategies and Skills for Successful Involvement in the Group

- Be here now
- Listen and reflect
- Initiate consistently to avoid fading into silence
- Monitor your personal process
- Learn to convey and receive feedback
- Track your awareness, discovery, and learning by keeping a journal

2

Early Middle Stage

MAJOR MEMBER CHALLENGES IN THE EARLY MIDDLE STAGE

The middle stage is a transitional stage in which the group begins to move toward productive work. However, conflict is a prevalent emotional feature of groups moving from beginning stages into the middle (working) stages (Bennis & Shepard, 1956, 1970; Bion, 1961; Corey, M.S. & Corey, G., 2006; Donigian & Malnati, 1997; Kline, 2003; Schutz, 1966; Tuckman, 1965; Yalom, 1995). It is likely that group members have long since learned to recognize patterns of avoidance (also referred to as flight) and external group boundary violations in topic selection by this time. Nonetheless, over time, perhaps through a few early sessions, their disillusionment with the leader leads members to conclude that he or she will never fulfill their needs. Usually, members have become aware of their dependence on the leader by now, but their awareness that their dependence has borne little if any fruit has been frustrating. This frustration leads to a change in some members' attitudes from submissive dependence to more counterdependent ones. Thus, members more actively display counterdependent and rebellious behavior and, subsequently, factions and pairings begin to emerge in the group (Bennis & Shepard, 1970).

CHARACTERISTICS OF THE EARLY MIDDLE STAGE: HELPFUL THINGS TO NOTICE

The rise of factions within the group becomes more evident as members begin choosing sides. Noticing this behavior will provide assistance in identifying which stage the group is in. Most, but not all, of the members split off into one or the other of two subgroups. One side continues its attempts to bring structure to the group and fill the apparent leadership gap. The other side takes opposition to every "structure-seeking" initiative. As this fragmentation continues to increase, group members target and blame the leader for his or her incompetence and the group's lack of progress as well.

Surprisingly, it is from this chaotic situation that something new and hopeful begins to emerge. Donigian and Malnati (1997) support this hopefulness and likewise predict that members will engage in behavior that signals the emergence of trust in this stage. Within factions that were sometimes at war with each other in the group, new alliances form and, to the astonishment of members, bonds of friendship and mutual support are forged. As alliances and bonds develop between factions that were formerly at war, another unanticipated challenge occurs. A new faction constituted by members whom Bennis and Shepard (1970) refer to as *independents* begins to emerge. The independents, less ambivalent toward authority than members of either other subgroup, hold more objective views, particularly concerning disagreements in the group. Their tendency is to take the role of the group leader and his or her interpretation of surfacing issues in the group at face value. Occasionally, independent members may even attempt to mediate group disputes but are usually unsuccessful because of their lacking bond with members of the other factions.

EARLY MIDDLE STAGE GROUP CHALLENGES: GOOD THINGS FOR YOU AS A MEMBER TO NOTICE

The major challenge for the group in the early middle stage is to weather the storm and sustain itself as a working unit. *Sustain* means that the group does not disintegrate in the face of continuing anxiety and new emerging tensions. Even though the group is no longer in the beginning stage, some members may still struggle to understand who they are within the group context. Others may also still grapple with questions about whether or not they can trust the group as a place to make themselves or their problems known.

Even though you may have begun to adjust to the ambiguity and anxiety that characterize the early stages of group life, the emergence of conflict may bring you yet another personal challenge depending on your ability to remain alert and keep yourself in balance when tension in the group is high. Even though the life of an effective group member is not supposed to be tortuous, you are likely seeing that the group is a social environment with its own culture and norms that strongly influence interpersonal relationships among and between members. Within its context, you have also likely begun to see how members express their unique personalities and begin to discover their shared connections. Also, you may begin to see how members seek ways to preserve a sense of personal worth while acknowledging the unique worth of others, the importance of the group, as well as the common good. All the while the life of the group unfolds, anxiety is in the picture. Sometimes it is in the background, at other times in the fore.

In the early middle stage, conflict also begins to emerge where before some group members choked back their frustrations while they looked for help from the leader. Others may have wondered why some members looked to the leader instead of to them. Perhaps some members (known as *personals*) seemed to always be wanting personal connection, whereas others (the *counterpersonals*) wondered why emphasis should be placed on making interactions so "touchy-feely," especially because they didn't come to the the group to "fall in love with everybody."

Reflecting on How You Deal With Anxiety and Conflict

Have you been scared off by the ambiguity? How are you with the conflict that may be emerging in your group now? If you notice member disagreements happening and the emergence of factions, where are you in all of it? Do you recognize that conflict can be beneficial? Have you been able to make conflict your friend? Kline (2003) makes a useful observation about groups and the ambiguity-conflict duo when he says, "Conflict is associated with members' attempts and inescapable failure to avoid anxiety" (p. 51).

Now is a good time to return to self-assessment and ask yourself some questions about how you are dealing with the ebb and flow of the group and the challenges it has brought so far. With regard to the climate that prevails at any moment, are you able to notice what it is and feel its impact by way of its expansion, diminishment, or shifts? Are you able to assess the climate of the group and monitor your internal reactions for clues as to what may be happening in the group?

By now you likely are able to make distinctions between patterns of fight and flight, which is to say that you are able to address what needs to be happening, especially in the face of whatever anxiety you or other group members may feel versus escaping to the past or some more comfortable topic, denying the anxiety, buying into the press of what will happen if you enter into revealing your unexpressed concerns, and resisting the work to be done.

You likely have a collection of first impressions and ideas about the personalities assembled in your group. What have you come to understand about what is expected of the group and what is expected of you? You have also probably discovered what the norms or guidelines are for effectiveness in your group. How about the group's maintenance of external boundaries and its work in the here and now? How did you discover what expectations exist in the group regarding norms and boundaries? What have you noticed about how others in your group are making discoveries? If discovery is not happening, if norms are lacking, what do you make of that?

The middle working stage presents a host of opportunities and possibilities for you. There is still time for you and the group. There are great possibilities for coming to life in this stage. Launch your boat now. Bon voyage!

EARLY MIDDLE STAGE MEMBER CHALLENGES: MORE GOOD THINGS FOR YOU TO NOTICE

The main personal challenge for you as a member within the context of group-level challenges of this stage is that you make an effort to maintain your effectiveness, keep yourself in balance, and not allow yourself to be overwhelmed by the complexity of issues or frustration and tension that are sometimes apparent in the group. Do not fear taking a risk to confront someone and do not fear being confronted. Do not buy into self-blame about the conflict, alignments that occur, or the extent to which you are a power for change or not in the group. Especially do not become too self-absorbed if you see yourself doing well in handling the change or even being facilitative in the face of it. Also, do not become overly self-critical with change in yourself, especially if you perceive it to be difficult to realize or happening more slowly in yourself than you prefer.

The major challenge for group members in the early middle stage is to stay the course in the midst of the stormy activity that may be happening in the group. Members will be forced to decide whether or not to stand alone or become a part of the group. As I have attempted to make clear, the aspects of conflict and its potential resolution involve new and surprising interactions among and between members as each member attempts to find his or her initiative and his or her fit in the balance of power that is developing in the group. Members also face the challenge of recognizing themes that touch upon their personal experiences and life hopes. Members also come to understand that many hopes, fears, frustrations, and tensions are held in common by other members of the group.

Another aspect of your personal challenge as a member in this stage is that you notice your place in the group. This is particularly important with regard to emerging factions and the developing hierarchy and group pecking order. It is also very important that you understand the "independent" personality type in the group, such as I have tried to give a hint of in the casting of Youtu and Ria in the scenarios. If that happens to be you, you should then understand that it likely means that you as a member have remained, for the most part, uncommitted to any subgroup. Thus, you have an additional personal dilemma to address because members who do not commit themselves to one or the other subgroup are ineffectual at best in their attempts to resolve existing conflict.

It is important for you to take the initiative to communicate your feelings and reactions about the state of the group, its atmosphere and alignments, and how and where you want to fit. In other words, take the risk of making your private wishes, hopes, feelings, and desires public in the group.

EARLY MIDDLE STAGE SCENARIOS

Early Middle Stage: Intersession Scenario Update (Sessions 2 and 3)

The group is approaching Session 4 and the beginning of the middle working stage. Although the group's Session 2 had been active, with many good things happening, much was also left unaddressed. Session 2 is the session in which you surprised yourself and other group members when you blurted out words to the following effect: "Can somebody tell me what the heck we're doing here?" Rick, the leader, picked up on your question immediately. It seemed that the aim of his response was to clarify your feelings of nervousness, anxiousness, and hesitancy about expressing your thoughts and feelings. It also seemed that you wanted direction for yourself and others in the group.

Unfortunately, Bill jumped in before you could respond to Rick and this created another problem, which may possibly have been an opportunity for you. When Bill said that he didn't need anybody to tell him what to do and that he could take care of himself just fine, you believed that he was directing his words and his angry tone to you because he took you as an easier "target" than the leader. Later, when the group was over, you realized that you had been "hooked" by Bill's attitude and his words because they played into feelings that are connected to your family history. Until now these feelings have been unaddressed.

With regard to overall group progress, Tony had been a central person in Session 2 because Doreen noticed that the group had gotten away from his expressed concerns. In the session, Ria was the most expressive of several members who reacted to Tony. She let him know that she had empathy for his pain even though she did not know its origin at the time. Ria connected with Tony's analogy of seeing the planet like a sinking ship aboard which he hoped he would not drown. She also told Tony that she saw him as a good guy. Tony had listened to Ria's remarks and appeared to be genuinely touched by her actions. He looked into her face all the while she spoke to him, but during that session he did not utter a single word in response. Nonetheless, members ended Session 2 with a sense of progress.

During Session 3, group members returned to some topics that were not fully completed in Session 2. Tony was the first person to speak. He directed most of his words to Ria and as he talks, the group discovers more about who he is. Tony further discloses to Ria and the group that he was born of a Vietnamese mother and African American father during the Vietnam War in 1967. His father, a recipient of the Silver Star, married his mother after his discharge and brought her and baby Tony to the United States. At age 6, Tony's grandmother in Vietnam became ill and his mother returned there with him to care for her and then came back to the United States. At age 7, Tony lost his mother to bomb-related cancer. At age 11, he lost his father to a freak car accident. Tony was remanded into the custody of his paternal grandmother, whom he lost to diabetes at age 13. He was then left in the care of a vicious, mean, and hateful aunt, the sister of his father's mother. The group was shocked by Tony's story and deeply moved. Until now, no one knew that Tony's father was an African American man. Tony's skin color was brown but his features appeared more Asian than African. Tony accepted much empathy and care from Ria but was very hostile toward the leader, Rick. Most group members found this odd because Rick had been the most compassionate toward him. Tony offered no explanation for his hostility toward Rick during the session.

During Session 3, you managed to find your voice again when Bill aligned strongly with Tony in his hostile feelings against Rick. You brought up your feelings about Bill's misdirected anger toward you, which you believed was actually intended for Rick. You also challenged Bill about his feelings for Ria and your hunch that he wished Ria's caring was directed to him instead of Tony. Bill quickly denied your suspicions, but when Ria challenged him because of his frequent "sneaky" eye contact, Bill said, "Maybe there's something to what you're saying, but I'm really not ready to go into it now." Bill then switched topics and reverted to a past discussion from Session 2 in which Rick made comments to the group about its talk about the weather and Hollywood actors that he thought to be missing the target.

Bill's words struck a defensive chord in the group with the members who had been a part of that discussion. Members reacted by pointing out Bill's "negative attitude" in the group "since day one," as Doreen reminded everyone how Bill had spent almost the entire first two sessions slumped down in his chair. Chris then spoke up on Bill's behalf to remind opponents that Bill had expressed sympathy for Tony early on, even if his comments were not expressed in the "proper group work" form. José then said to Chris, "I don't see that there's anything so great about Bill's reaction to Tony. Bill is like a ventriloquist who speaks through other people. The problem is, though, that you never really know what his message is." The scowl that took over Bill's face suggested that he was infuriated by José's words. "Man, you just need to shut up," Bill said. "You don't even know what you're talking about. Where do you get off calling me a ventriloquist? I don't know where you're coming from with that." The tension in the group was apparent, but José did not back down. There is not enough time to address the conflict emerging between José and Bill, but before the session ended there was an out-and-out verbal fight between two small clusters in the group. Bill, Tony, and Chris composed one cluster and José, Doreen, and Jewels composed the other. You and Ria seemed to be out of the action. Session 3 appeared to end in an unresolved standoff between the two clusters.

Early Middle Stage Challenges: Scenario 4

As the group begins Session 4, the atmosphere is tense. Bill immediately picks up on José's remarks from the last session and demands a further explanation from him regarding his comments about him being like a ventriloquist.

"From what I see," José calmly says

> the first time Tony spoke, you rode in on his feelings, saying that you could relate to his pain and you agreed that the world is a freaking mess. Then you rode in again on Youtu's words when he/she asked what the heck was happening? You responded with words like, "I don't need nobody to tell me what the heck to do 'cause I can take care of myself just fine." Personally, I think Youtu was right. Even though your words really appeared to be meant for Rick, you gave your anger to Youtu.

José's words and calm delivery are almost too much for Bill to take. His face flushes red and it is hard for most members to know if he is angry or embarrassed. Suddenly Bill stands up from his chair and says, "I'm outta here." When he turns to leave the room, Tony speaks up and says, "Think about it, man." Bill's expression turned to exasperation as he says, "I hear you man, but I'm just not fitting in here." Chris then passes an unopened bottle of water to Bill and says, "We all get thirsty in the desert or when our ship is lost at sea." Bill does appear to be lost as he stands there. Tony picks up on Chris' language and says to Bill, "How about sitting down, Bro?"

Bill surveys the group and all eyes are upon him. Every face reflects concern but Bill turns around and rushes for the door. Ria shouts, "Man overboard!" Rick immediately sprints after Bill and most of the other group members stand up from their seats. Ria walks toward the door but decides not to go out after Bill.

The group members wonder what will happen next because Bill has now left the group. However, Rick is standing with him just outside the door of the group's meeting room. Ria decides to wait inside. She asks Rick for a chance to speak with Bill before he leaves, if he decides to go. Outside, Rick is attempting to get Bill to delay his decision. "Maybe you will decide that you don't want to be in this group," Rick says, "but if I had to judge by the expressions on the faces of everyone in that room, I'd say that even though every one of them doesn't like your attitude and how you say the things you have to say, no one of them wants you out of the group. I think it would be great to learn more about what makes you feel satisfied or not about how you are fitting into the group."

Bill responds by saying, "To tell you the truth, you are someone I don't fit with. You seem like a fairly okay man, Rick, but I don't fit with you." Rick shrugs his shoulders and says, "What does 'don't fit' mean?" Bill's jaw line shows tension as he answers. "I really don't know," he says. "I don't know what the issue is. I just know that when certain people want you to fix stuff ... like fix the group or tell us what to do, I just can't relate to that." "I noticed," Rick says, "but I think we'll probably figure it out if you stick around. How about it?" Bill begins to look bewildered. "But how can I face these people?" Bill asks. "And that José ... I'm not sure I can keep it together with him. Man, that guy takes me right to the edge."

"Well," says Rick. "I'm sure you don't need *me* to tell you the answer, right? But I would like to ask you something." "Go for it," Bill says. Then Rick says, "What about Ria? Shall I tell her you drowned or what? I mean do you need my help with that?"

Bill cracks his first smile since the group began and he lets out a sigh as he says, "Touché, Mr. Rick. No, I don't need your help with Ria. Just give me a second or two. I'll be back inside in a few."

When Rick steps back into the meeting room alone, all the members look toward the door. Chris looks to Ria and then to Rick and says, "Did we lose him?" "I think he's deciding," says Rick. Then Tony mumbles, "Study long and you'll study wrong." Seconds later, Bill steps back into the room. Everyone applauds and Ria, who is sitting on the sidelines near the door, stands and says, "Good choice. Welcome back, Bill." Then she walks back to her chair in the circle.

Before Rick is seated, Doreen says, "I'm really glad you went after Bill. I was worried that no one would do anything." Before Rick can make any response, José speaks up and says, "I don't know why we expect so much from Rick. He obviously wants us to figure it out on our own." Doreen retorts, "You mean you wonder why 'you' expect so much from Rick." José pauses for a moment and says, "Yeah, I guess I should 'own' my opinion. I do think I expect a lot, but I think some others expect a lot too." Quizzical expressions come over the faces of Doreen and Jewels. José chuckles then says, "I won't say any names, but I will give the initials of at least two people, which are Doreen and Jewels." Before either Doreen or Jewels can respond, Bill jumps into the fray and says, "You two are busted—you might just as well take ownership of that 'cause you two are always looking at Rick like you need him to tell you whether or not to breathe."

Doreen throws a pillow, which Bill catches and then says in a mock-female voice, "Umm. Rick, can I hold this pillow? Should I toss it back at Billy or should I just squeeze it till our session ends today?" Then Jewels speaks up and playfully says to Bill, "I think it would be great if you just opened wide and stuffed it into that cavern of a mouth you've got." Tony releases a spontaneous "Oh-ooo!" Then Rick intervenes.

> I'm not entirely sure how group members have felt about my leadership in the past, but it seems like the group is definitely making some decisions about its leadership right now. I see members connecting themselves to the group and choosing to share more and more often. I'm seeing a lot of honesty too. Some of it is tempered—maybe even covered up by joking and sarcasm but everyone here seems to be able to recognize and feel the truth that's coming through. It looks like you have the resources among yourselves to provide whatever help the group may need.

Even though you have been a very quiet member again in this session, you have observed Bill and the group closely and you stood up with others when Bill left the room. You don't see yourself as a part of either subgroup. You are not sure that the subgroups even see themselves as subgroups, but it is clear to you that they do exist. You take the opportunity to let everyone know that you do not want Bill to leave the group, but when you attempt to give your opinion about Rick's leadership of the group, no one seems to listen. Members continue talking as if you had not spoken. Some even talk over your words when you attempt to say anything.

Intersession Scenario Update: (Early Middle Stage Session 5)

As the group approached Session 6, it had progressed to the near end of the early middle stage. The two subgroups that started to emerge in Session 3 continued to make connections and strong bonds had begun to form. During Session 4, the two groups were increasingly more verbal and active, with the result that Session 5 was a highly significant session for the group. During Session 5, Rick announced to the group that he was withdrawing into a nonleader position in the group. He explained to the group that he was making this choice because of repeated challenges to his role as the leader. He mentioned that there were complaints about his failure to provide adequate guidance and complaints that in some instances he was manipulative and secretly controlling the group.

After announcing his decision, Rick turned the leadership responsibility completely over to the group. He said that he would remain present but not take up any leadership responsibilities unless the majority of group members requested such assistance. After the members adjusted to the shock of Rick's announcement, even though he had given a hint at the end of Session 4, the group took itself through most of the meeting with no apparent help from Rick. The group spent most of its time discussing Rick's announcement and issues of dependence and conflict. Members were generally quite forthright and honest. Several members, including Tony, Doreen, José, and Chris, expressed appreciation for feedback that gave them insights into member perceptions regarding their orientations toward authority and personal relations. The group seemed to experience a powerful sense of coalescence and members were surprised that such understanding and closeness could develop among people who were strangers only four weeks before. As

Rick observed the events from the proverbial sideline, the group ended Session 5 on a very upbeat note.

Early Middle Stage: Scenario 6

The strong feelings of warmth and connection discovered by group members in Session 5 carry over into the now current Session 6. Rick has returned to the circle, at least in physical terms, but he makes no attempt to further discuss or clarify his role when he takes his seat. In some ways, his posture is reminiscent of the first meetings of the group, but the atmosphere this time is entirely different. During this meeting, you venture forth again to say how helpful the recent group discussion has been. You share with the group how you came to realize how much you expected Rick's help when you first came into the group. You also confess to the group that reading one of the articles suggested by Rick helped you to see yourself more clearly in terms of expectations for structure and guidance from the leader.

José ventures forth to say how frustrating the first group meetings were as he and others seemed to try and make sense of what was supposed to happen. Jewels mentions how lost she had felt but also speaks to Bill. "Something about your attitude was catchy, Bill," she says. "What I saw as your aloof persona made me take a look at myself." Bill sits up in his seat. "It's funny, Jewels, that you reacted to me that way because I had no idea how I was coming across, but it wasn't long before Ria's comments helped me to realize that my behavior was really over the top." Then Tony joins in. He turns to Rick and says, "A comment that you made ... something about family group recapitulation or something like that, really clicked with me. I started to see how much I was influenced by things in my earlier family life." José, Doreen, and Chris spontaneously share that they have gained a lot of insight, too, because they each knew that they had a lot of "family baggage." Then you tell Chris that you appreciate her sharing because you had hopes of getting to know more about her. You also tell her that you find her sense of timing in the group really effective in creating movement. You give her the example of her comment when passing a bottle of water to Bill in his moment of distress.

Bill, who has been rather quiet during this session, makes a disclosure that surprises most of the group.

> You folks may not believe it, but I want you to know that I've gotten some insights into some stuff I need to work on too. It has to do with how I feel about some kinds of men. See, my dad was a nice guy and Rick, you reminded me of him when I first came to the group. I was angry with myself that I didn't bring it up in the screening interview because then I would have known more about what I was getting into. I guess I'm not all that clear about what I want to say because I really believe that you are a nice guy, Rick. See, my dad only *seemed* nice because behind closed doors at home, he was a monster. So this is why I have problems with you.

Rick simply nods through Bill's disclosure. He seems to have taken in a lot but he doesn't reply in words. Then Chris speaks up. "I want to say something," she says. She looks at Maria and smiles a big smile. "You, Ria," she says, "I appreciate you a lot because you remind me of my big sister, Katie. In my family, she was my hero and she was my safety net … just like I think you are for Bill in the group."

Early Middle Stage Scenario 6: Alternative Ending A

There is a lull in the group after Chris's remarks and Doreen begins to speak. She brings the group's attention to something she had not mentioned since the first group meeting but never talked about since then. "Things that have happened in our last few sessions," she says,

> and especially things like those that came up in our last session, and like some of the things like what we've heard just now heard from Bill, really make me realize how judgmental my family is. My mother is a judger and I think that one of reasons I avoid you, Bill, is because I see you as a judger, too. When we were first beginning the group and I told about my father's affair and the brother who was born from it, I thought you were judging me and judging everyone else, when you slumped down in your chair. To be honest, I really had no idea what you were doing, but judging you was easier for me than asking. When I saw this in myself, I couldn't believe it. Then I realized something else … that I never heard my father's side of the story. I listened to my mother and, secretly, I judged my dad. I don't know what caused my dad to fall in love with another woman, but I do know that I judged him like my mother did. And I judged the child who is my brother and I never even met him. Since I've been in this group, I haven't liked myself very much at all. I'm starting to get sick of judging others 'cause its robbing me of my life.

For the second time since the group began, Doreen has everyone's attention. Rick looks around the group and everyone is in the moment. Even Bill is sitting up in his chair. Tony gets up from his chair and crosses the room. He sits on the floor next to Doreen and says "It's really great to hear from you. I appreciate what you've shared and I have a new opinion of you tonight. I guess I've been judging you unconsciously because I wasn't learning much about you and I never took a chance to ask. I'm sorry about that, Doreen." Then Rick says, "I've wondered about you too, Doreen. I don't think that I'm a judger but I have wanted to hear more from you. I like what I've heard tonight." Then Rick looks around the group and says, "I wonder how other folks are feeling? We're just about to run out of time. Does anybody have any reactions or anything they'd like to share?" Chris speaks up and says to Doreen,

> I really can't tell you how much the things you have said meant to me today. I have felt judged a lot in my life and judgments of others against me, especially in my family, have caused me a lot of pain. So I just wanted to let you know that it touched me a lot to see you take ownership for being a judger like your mom. I also want to say that I hope you talk to your dad sometime and I hope that you meet your brother.

Early Middle Stage Scenario 7: Alternative Ending B

At the beginning of Session 7, Doreen enters the group filled with so much excitement that she is hardly able to contain herself. After having followed Chris's suggestion that she talk to her father, Doreen is beaming. She discloses to the group how she told her dad that she believed she had judged him because that was the example she had gotten from her mother. She also tells the group how she had confessed to her father, Angelo, the dismay she had felt for judgments she had made against him without knowing the full story. Doreen explained to the group that her father and mother divorced when she was 6 years old and that she was greatly attached to him. He, too, loved her very much and continued regular contact with her. Her father then told her that even though her brother was born out of wedlock, he was not born of an extramarital affair. Her father began dating the child's mother, Celeste, a year after having been divorced and, in fact, hoped to marry her. After the first year of their relationship, Celeste feared that she and Angelo would be overwhelmed by the stresses of an interracial marriage in the community and times in which they lived. Further, she did not believe that Angelo would be acceptable in her parents' eyes, especially not in those of her father because of the strict traditional Southern African American family background from which he came. Based on these things, Celeste and Angelo argued incessantly. Angelo tried to convince Celeste that a marriage could work, in spite of her fatalistic speculation. But Celeste was relentless in her expressed point of view and, finally, she pronounced the relationship to be over. Angelo was shattered. Celeste moved away to an unknown location without giving her former fiancé any idea as to where she had gone. He inquired with her family but they would not volunteer any details.

Two years after Angelo had "moved on," so he thought, he learned that Celeste was pregnant at the time they had separated. She had never informed him that he now had a son, Luke, who was a little more than one year old. Angelo shared with Doreen how heart-rending it was to discover this news about Celeste. He also shared that he had been deeply in love with Celeste, but that he had also loved Doreen's mother, Becky. He explained that he never chose one woman over the other and was only trying to have a life with both his children. Needless to say, Doreen was tremendously moved by the story and by her father's trust after she had confessed having judged him without knowing his side.

After sharing her story, Doreen is warmly embraced by Jewels and supported by the group with hugs, smiles, loving remarks, and pats on the back. Throughout Doreen's disclosure, Chris is withdrawn and has begun to sink down into her chair. Several members inquire as to how she is, but no one is able to budge her from her obvious sullen posture. Unbeknownst to the group, Chris had seen Tony and Ria having coffee in the supermarket café, but they had not seen her. She did not approach them, she only ran away upset as if she had discovered two people having an affair. However, Tony and Ria had already decided to tell the group about their chance meeting in the store. Tony tells the group how much he hated to shop but had gone to this particular store because a friend had told him that he could find an extraordinary kind of noodles, which he liked, in that store. "I went in there just to grab up some of those noodles," said Tony. "Then I was going to be out of there, but who do I bump into but Ria. So I asked her to have coffee with me there in the store and she agreed. I wasn't looking to go out on a date. In fact, both of us are dating others, but I like Ria, I respect her, and I view her as a friend and valuable member of our group." Tony went on to explain how he shared with Ria some of his impressions of her in the group. Ria in turn shared some of her impressions of Tony. She and Tony realized that they had become a subgroup, so they agreed not to share their secret hopes in the café but instead they chose to wait and do that sharing in the group. They even thought of how to use their secrets as bargaining chips to get other members of the group to risk sharing their secret hopes and fears.

Tony laughed as he looked at Chris and said, "What I want to know from you is the secret of why you've been slumping down in your chair like Bill today. Is something happening with you? I noticed that you barely spoke to me when we were near the vending machines just before the meeting today." Chris continues to slump without looking in Tony's direction, but after a very long pause, she says,

> I'm real embarrassed and I think I'm discovering that I've got some issues that I don't know how to talk about. I'm glad that you and Ria said the things you did because I saw you in the café but I hid. I don't know why but I didn't want you to know that I saw you. I guess if I did then I would've had to deal with some of the crazy feelings I had, like if Ria likes you … and really to me, it seems like in this group she always has … then that would mean I would lose her friendship to you.

Tony throws his hands up as if someone has approached him with a gun. "It's really not like that," he says. "I never had the idea that Ria is my property or that I have any exclusive rights to her friendship. Besides, I already told you that both of us have significant others right now. I really don't get what's happening with you and these 'crazy feelings' you mentioned. Can you tell me more about those feelings?"

Ria speaks up and says, "I consider you as my friend and group mate, Chris, but I'm completely puzzled by your ideas about losing my friendship with you. Can you talk to me … to us about it? I really am surprised and very confused. … I mean totally, you know?"

Chris sits up in her chair, but she makes no eye contact. She appears to be studying the small squares in the carpet. Finally, she says, "I thought I was coming to this group to improve my relationship skills, but now I think I've totally failed."

Bill speaks up as Chris is looking bewildered and says, "What I want to know, Chris, is whatever happened to your sister who was always your safety net? The one that Ria reminds you of?" Chris is silent for a long time, then her eyes began to tear. Choking back tears she says in an unsteady voice,

> Katie was my safety net, but she left me too. But it was my fault. She took me in when I was twelve. My dad didn't want me and mom was an alcoholic. Katie took me in to live with her. I was a big responsibility for her and she was only twenty-two. I was a sickly kid, plus I had asthma. I lost my inhaler on the way home from school, but I didn't tell Katie. I thought I could sneak out and find it but that night I had an attack. When I told Katie that I lost my inhaler, she rushed out of the apartment to the pharmacy and … and … she … she never came back.

Chris then began to quietly weep and through her tears, she moaned, "Katie was killed in a car accident on the way back from the pharmacy."

A sorrowful sigh is heaved by the listeners, who move from their seats to be closer to Chris. Rick, who is two members to her left, says in a clear and solemn voice,

> Perhaps you do have issues, Chris, but whatever they are they cannot be dealt with until you recognize one monumental truth and it is this: Katie's death is not your fault. Can you say this sentence, Chris? "Katie did not choose to leave me and her death was not my fault." Every one of us is here to help you Chris. Whenever you are ready, please try and say the words.

An otherworldly expression drifts across Chris's face. It appears to be some mixture of astonishment, relief, and disbelief. She smiles an absent-looking smile and whispers, "I ... never, ever, thought about it like you're saying, Rick. I always believed it was my fault. My dad always said that nothing went right when I was around. From the day I was born, nothing was ever right again in his life, he said, and that was my entire fault."

"Your father is another issue," Rick says. "Let's stay with your sister Katie for now. Can you say these words: 'Katie did not choose to leave me and her death was not my fault'?" Chris pauses for a few seconds then she slowly begins to recite Rick's sentence: "Katie did not choose to leave me and her death was not my fault."

"Can you repeat it again, Chris?" Rick asks. Ria kneels in front of Chris's chair and slowly shakes her head. Chris begins to say the words: "Katie did not choose to leave me and her death was not my fault." After Bill says the sentence two or three times, Ria joins his recitation with the sentence: "Katie did not choose to leave you and her death was not your fault." Then Tony joins in and repeats the words, then Bill, then José, then Doreen, then Jewels, Youtu, and Rick the leader all recite the sentence in cacophony beneath Chris's dawning recognition: "Katie did not choose to leave you, Chris, and her death was not your fault."

The session ends on a high note as Chris is provided an opportunity to reevaluate and begin to free herself from a burden she has carried for more than 10 years. She tells the group that she is leaving the session with a lot to think about. She says that she feels surprised at her sense of relief and that for the first time in a long while she feels hopeful, even though she knows that she still has a lot of work to do.

Doreen thanks the group for the support she received and gives a special thanks to Chris for the encouraging nudge that took her farther than she had imagined. No one says anything to Rick directly. Bill extends an open hand toward him for a handshake and every member in the room smiles at Rick. Each and every one of them says, "Good night, Rick," in a clearly audible voice that seems to be conveying, albeit even if in code, acknowledgment of Rick's positive contribution that night.

Multicultural Considerations: Early Middle Stage

During Session 2 in the intersession scenario update, Youtu blurts out the question, "Can somebody tell me what the heck we're doing here?" The leader, Rick, immediately recognizes that the question may be a possible attempt for Youtu to address and clarify unexpressed feelings of nervousness, anxiousness, and hesitancy. It is a double opportunity for Youtu. In the first instance, from the point of view of Bowman's (1996) multicultural training, the rather elusive Youtu has a chance to begin more active self-discovery, which is a prerequisite to working with others. In the second instance, in addition to learning about her- or himself, Youtu has a chance to learn about how she or he relates to others. Also, Bill's jumping into the fray before Youtu can respond and denying his own need for help convinces Youtu that Bill's words were just an indirect expression of anger toward the group leader. It is an insightful observation on Youtu's part.

Interpersonal learning continues to increase and accelerate during Sessions 2 and 3. Members not only make discoveries about fellow members' personalities, they also gain insights into fellow members' ethnic identities within their families of origin. Doreen notices that the group had dropped its attention toward Tony. Ria gives him feedback, and in Session 3, Tony is the first member to speak. He further discloses not only that he was born of a Vietnamese mother and American father but that his American father was an African American man who was highly decorated in the Army. Tony makes shocking disclosures about his personal suffering due to losses in his family. He also expresses some hostility toward Rick, the leader. However, Tony's hostile feelings were not explored in Session 3. From a multicultural perspective, Tony's presence and disclosures in the group are catalytic in that they foster awareness of the unseen aspects of identity, as well as the interaction of ethnicity, culture, skin color, and personal racial identity. As Session 3 progresses, there is increasing conflict in the group, but the source of the conflict is not apparent. Youtu finds her or his voice and tells Bill that the feelings he had aimed at Youtu seemed to be his angry feelings toward Rick. Youtu also confronted Bill about his feelings about Ria and his possible wish that more of her caring could be directed toward him instead of Tony. When Bill is confronted with feedback about his tendency to use many words and also switch topics frequently, two opposing subgroups emerge. The subgroups hold opposing opinions about Bill. Tension between the two subgroups is further exacerbated when José labels Bill as a ventriloquist who can only express his thoughts and feelings by talking through others. The fact that this conflict comes after Tony's powerful disclosures in the group makes it clear that there can be subterranean feelings and issues that affect the group. Attention to such feelings and issues through honest, self-aware exchanges and openness to discovery about who the other person is beyond one's limited idea or preconceived notion holds extraordinary potential for interpersonal and multicultural discovery and learning.

The group tension continues into Session 4. José launches a commentary on Bill's alleged "ventriloquism" in which he "piggybacks" or rides into the group discussion on the feelings expressed by others but not initiated by himself. Bill reacts by flushes of red to his face and neck but no words come forth. Although he does not say what his feelings are, members guess that he is exasperated and angered by José. When Bill decides to leave the room, several members react. Ria yells out: "Man overboard!" as Bill heads toward the door. Rick goes after Bill and convinces him to stay with the group. Bill agrees and is welcomed back to the group. Rick makes a positive mass group (group-focused) commentary but no apparent racial, ethnic, or cultural concerns are processed in the group at that time.

As the group moves through the intersession updates of Session 5, it is clear that during this session and the earlier Sessions 3 and 4, two subgroups have emerged and made their presence apparent to everyone. During this time, Youtu also recognized that she or he is an independent who does not belong to either subgroup. During this session, Rick withdraws from leadership and turns the responsibility over to the group. He agrees to remain but not take any leadership initiatives unless the majority of group members request it. Surprisingly, the group members discuss Rick's decision without conflict and without any apparent focus on Rick's race or color. The group actually moves forward during this time of change.

In Session 6, feelings of warmth are highly prevalent. Rick returns to the group as a member but still without attention to his leader role. In a surprise disclosure, Youtu confesses her or his discoveries, especially in terms of expectations of more help from the leader. As the group becomes more harmonious, seeing that it can survive, hold itself together, and weather conflict, more member disclosures are made. This development is instructive from the multicultural point of view because it shows that groups ordinarily need some preparatory level of readiness in order to effectively address and deal with the volatility of ethnicity and race-related concerns in the group. Rick had briefly discussed family group recapitulation, which describes how members' past experiences and expectations combine to recreate aspects of their family life in the group. Members respond, often unconsciously, as if they were parents, siblings, or other significant individuals from their original family constellations. Responses and ways of reacting and relating cover the entire spectrum of feelings from positive to negative, ranging from hostility and aggression to extraordinary empathy, intimacy, and love.

Later, Tony shares that Rick's comments helped him see how much impact experiences from his past family life had unknowingly affected him. He does not venture into an explanation of his hostile feelings toward Rick, but it is apparent that discovery and insight are turning about inside him nonetheless, like wheels. Again, from the multicultural point of view, it is clear that members are learning about themselves and learning about others, including how their ways of relating to one another are happening in the group. In fact, the self-discovery that is occurring is a powerful impetus toward improved interpersonal connection within the group. As members "see" more of how they are and how they see their past experiences in the context of the present, they gain insight into how they relate, not only to members of the group but, subsequently, how they relate to others in their worlds outside. These events lead to a growth explosion in the group. José, Doreen, and Chris spontaneously share that they, too, had gained insights into their own family baggage, which had gone largely unacknowledged until they joined the group. Bill, who had aligned with Tony in his expression of hostile feelings toward Rick, makes a surprising disclosure about his father's double faces, that he was nice in public but had been a monster at home. For Bill, Rick's "niceness" created ambivalence and a reminder of the untrustworthy niceness of his father. Finally, Chris, a young White woman, tells Ria, a young Black woman, that Ria reminds her of her sister because Ria is a hero in the group like her sister was a hero in her life.

In Alternate Ending A for Scenario 6, members continue to have exceptional insights into themselves through glimpses into how they behaved in the context of their families. Doreen gains highly significant insights into her struggle with discovering that her dad had fathered a son with a Black woman. When she saw similarities between herself and her mother as they relate to tendencies to level judgments against others without knowing the full facts, Doreen was humbled and embarrassed. Tony was moved by Doreen's courageous and risky honesty.

In the Alternate Ending B for Scenario 6, Doreen had taken her insight to action by visiting her father and discovering more about him after he was divorced from her mother. Doreen also discovered hugely important details about her father's prospective new partner and other circumstances regarding the birth of her biracial brother, Luke.

Chris, who has spotted Tony and Ria outside the group in a public café, discloses her fear of losing friendship with Ria because of her closeness to Tony. Some members wonder if there could be unknown aspects of Chris's sexual preferences, but Bill tunes into Chris's recent comments about how she compared Ria to her sister Katie and designated them both as heroes. Bill's initiative leads the group to discover that Katie had died in a car accident after rushing to the pharmacy to obtain an inhaler for asthma-ridden Chris. An extraordinary group closing happens as the group members support Chris and remind her that Katie's death was not her fault.

QUESTIONS FOR CHAPTER REVIEW

1. As you think about over the events of this group, which interactions are most memorable and stand out in your mind?
2. What do you think about Rick's decision to step back from his leader role? Does Rick's decision facilitate progress in the group?
3. In Rick's absence, what is the source of leadership in this stage?
4. In the role of Youtu, how effective are you as a member in this stage? What are you doing well? What could be better?
5. In your opinion, which group members appear to be most effective in this stage?
6. What signs do you see of growth and development happening in this group?
7. If you came forward in this group as the person you are now, what could you share from your own life?

PART 1 PROLOGUE TIPS FOR THE EARLY MIDDLE STAGE

Key Components of an Effective Member Mindset

Develop the Capacity to Handle Conflict and Confrontation

- Successful growth groups almost always experience conflict.
- Conflict may be intrapersonal, meaning that it is internal to yourself, or interpersonal, which means that it is between you and one or more other people.

- Experiential learning settings encourage interpersonal contact that immediately forces members into greater awareness of their boundaries. For this reason, conflict in groups may happen on more than one level.
- As a participant in a group, the mere fact of being placed in proximity to others will bring challenges related to "intimacy" and "authority."
- *Intimacy* refers to how you deal with closeness in relationships.
- *Authority* refers to how you deal with others whom you experience to be powerful.
- Privately held expectations about the extent to which your hopes will be realized or crushed lead to collective challenges for the group as a unit and will likely bring your own issues and those of others to the surface.

Keep in Mind the Interactive Processes of Group Work

- The central focus of group work is interpersonal. In other words, several people are together as a group and the focus is on what is happening among and between them.
- Donigian and Malnati (1997) hold the view that every therapy group consists of three elements: the member, the leader, and the group.
- Each element is considered to be essential to effective group work, but the real attention is on how transactions are exchanged among these elements of the group.
- Kline's (2003) acknowledgement of what he calls *core interpersonal issues* include involvement, dependency, authority, individuation, intimacy, and loss. The core interpersonal issues represent a group development schema in themselves.
- The core interpersonal issue confronted by the group at any particular time denotes the group's stage of development.
- An effective group member notices which issues and related themes are most prevalent in group interaction.
- It is helpful to notice what happens between yourself and the group leader, what happens between yourself and the group, and what happens to you within the context of the group as a unit or system.
- Hulse-Killacky, Killacky and Donigian's (2001) three questions will propel group members to greater involvement if they are honestly explored: Who am I? Who am I with you? Who are we together?

Learn How to Think in Process Terms and Distinguish Between Content and Process

- Content and process are a unity of two elements in interaction with each other. In group situations, they are always present together.
- In the context of interpersonal relationships, content and process usually occur simultaneously over a designated period of time.

- In effective groups where content and process are in balance, group members experience the content as inherently more dynamic and living, regardless of the nature of themes or topics.
- In other words, process is the activating cause of meaningful and facilitative interaction in groups.
- When groups are experienced as flat, slow-moving, and lacking energy, the explanation usually has to do with the process.
- In group work, content refers to the apparent topic or activity. Content is usually experienced in degrees of density while at the same time remaining external, obvious, and, for the most part, on the surface.
- Matters relating to content are likely to be visible or audible or both. The substance of this content may be perceived as negative, positive, or indifferent.
- The group member who is a widow telling the group about her parents' first date before getting married is an example in which the content will be the words of her story.
- Process refers to the less obvious energy or feeling that accompanies the content.
- Usually, matters relating to process are not visible or audible, but they are noticeable and clearly felt.

Understand the Purpose of the Group

- Through the process of interaction, you will have opportunities to gain counseling, self-awareness, and interpersonal counseling skills through the activities of the group.
- You will have many opportunities to discover things about yourself in terms of what your strengths are in relationship with others and what the impacts of your communication style are.
- You are also likely to discover things about your power as well as your fears.
- You will have a chance to acquire strategies for dealing with challenges and crises in your life, being more productive in situations of conflict, and fostering growth and positive change in others.

Understand Expectations Relating to Safety

- You can expect to be safe in the group.
- You have a right to expect that you will not be physically harmed.
- You should understand that if you threaten the physical safety of others, you will be removed from the group.

Check Your Attitude

- A thoughtful assessment (and reassessment) of your frame of mind as you enter the group and as you begin each session can be very helpful.

- Have you been mandated or required to attend for some personal or health-related reason? If you are coming into the group with the feeling of being forced, it may still be helpful for you to acknowledge your unwillingness, lack of interest, or resistance and attempt to reframe them.
- In other words, it might be helpful to try using your unwillingness to your own advantage and to that of the group as well.
- It may be helpful to understand that your personal feelings and reactions can be keys to your effectiveness.
- If you are entering the group because you are genuinely interested in discovering more about yourself, about how to deal with the unique challenges of your life and circumstances, and interested to know about how others see you, that will make it all the better.

Open Yourself to Discovery

- Openness refers to our personal accessibility, meaning the extent to which you are willing to share, reveal, or disclose what you believe, fear, feel, or hope for; what you want or need; what you do well or poorly; and what you like or dislike about yourself.
- Also relevant in openness is your willingness to share feelings, thoughts, and attitudes you hold about others.
- Know that you are not expected to be completely vulnerable and helpless in the group.
- It is not "openness at any cost" but rather what I like to think of as *constructive openness*.
- Constructive openness involves risk and benefit. You are continuously choosing and taking chances one moment at a time. What you face may be exhilarating or horrifying.
- However, understanding more about the impact of your presence and personality, power, weaknesses, and strengths, about your lovability, and talent is the kind of discovery that groups have to offer.

PART 2 PROLOGUE TIPS FOR THE EARLY MIDDLE STAGE

Basic Strategies and Skills for Successful Involvement in the Group

- Remember to remember
- Be here now
- Learn to convey and receive feedback
- Express feelings as feelings
- Initiate consistently to avoid fading into silence
- Monitor your personal process
- Utilize the three-lenses approach
- Track your awareness, discovery, and learning by keeping a journal

3

Late Middle Stage

MAJOR MEMBER CHALLENGES IN THE LATE MIDDLE STAGE

The transition from conflict to cohesion is addressed by several authors, all of whom characterize movement from the early middle into the late middle stage by observable changes in the "emotional feeling quality" of the group (Bennis & Shepard, 1956; Corey, M.S. & Corey, G., 2006; Donigian & Malnati, 1997; Kline, 2003; Tuckman, 1965; Yalom, 1995). In the late middle stage the group begins to address its internal conflict more directly than ever before. Sometimes the warmth of closeness and newly discovered connections from the end of the earlier stage carries over and group members continue to hold onto the exuberant sense of beginning to feel understood. Interaction addresses fears related to rejection, acceptability, vulnerability, and exposure. Even though everything is not "coming up roses," group members have more familiarity with the surprising varieties of tension and shifts in anxiety that happen in the group. They have survived conflict and arguments and made many discoveries about how to survive "stormy" weather and close contact, even when it is tinged with a confrontational feeling. In those cases where combat is a possibility, and it does remain a possibility, members have had the experience of seeing alliances form between oppositional subfactions and bonds form where one would not have expected them to occur. Thus, members understand the unpredictable growth potential of conflict and discontent and regardless of their orientations to personal relations, intimacy, and closeness are always in the picture in some way.

CHARACTERISTICS OF THE LATE MIDDLE STAGE: HELPFUL THINGS TO NOTICE

The implications for you as a member in the context of this stage are that you remain vigilant and active in conveying and soliciting feedback. It will be helpful for you to notice when and at what times you feel connections with others in the group. It will also be helpful to keep your "thermometer" handy so that you can monitor what the group's atmosphere and temperature are like. The climate of the group in this stage, when acting in combination with the collective experience of the group, frequently leads to deepening levels of intimacy, self-selected vulnerability, and highly emotional and intense personal sharing. The openness of expression in this stage sometimes leads to conflict about the extent and degree to which one should be emotionally accessible and close to others. Thus, you will be affected by the risks and disclosures that your fellow group members make. You will have to consider the extent to which you feel ready and willing to share in similar or even more risky, self-exposing, and self-challenging ways than your peers. Not that it is a self-sharing contest. It is simply that you may find new possibilities for self-discovery in the universal themes that are uncovered in issues confronted and revealed by members in this stage. Where there may have been factions in the earlier stages vying for complete harmony no matter what, now there is emerging potential in the group-wide support and tolerance for differing views concerning how things in the group should be. After having seen the incredible interconnectedness of the themes of group members' lives, you will possibly be moved to reflect upon the extent you feel secure enough to deepen your level of sharing and involvement with others in the group and ask yourself a question that you will be continually brought face to face with in the group: To what extent am I willing, by my risk and sharing, to permit others to know who I am?

LATE MIDDLE STAGE GROUP CHALLENGES: GOOD THINGS FOR YOU AS A MEMBER TO NOTICE

The major challenge in the late middle stage is to productively explore contact and closeness while sustaining collective self-direction as a unit. As I have mentioned earlier, several authors characterize this stage primarily by its emotional intensity (Bennis & Shepard, 1956; Corey, M.S. & Corey, G., 2006; Donigian & Malnati, 1997; Kline, 2003; Tuckman, 1965; Yalom, 1995). Even though there is some recycling and reemergence of challenges that have been faced in earlier stages related to anxiety and conflict, there is an apparent increase in emotional feeling and capacity within the group, to live and work in the here and now—to be present and make significant connection in depth. As the group moves well into the late middle stage, the type of enchantment the group had known at the end of the early middle stage, in which there was much sweetness and lightness, begins to fade. The idyllic, "group is embracing us all" enchantment is replaced by enchantment with members' new subfactions. The two subfactions, which appear to challenge the idea of collective group direction, are usually divided between members of either counterpersonal or overpersonal orientation. However, both these subfactions are engaged in fighting against anxieties and tension related to intimacy aspects of intermember relations. This development marks the beginning of the subphase dubbed *disenchantment* by Bennis and Shepard (1970). Thus, Kline

(2003) and a host of other authors support the view of this stage as one where the major work of the group centers around intimacy concerns (Bennis & Shepard, 1956, 1970; Bion, 1961; Corey, M.S. & Corey, G., 2006; Donigian & Malnati, 1997; Schutz, 1966; Yalom, 1995). This struggle, which Bennis and Shepard (1970) refer to as a *theme*, would in their view likely be voiced by the group as "if others really knew me, they would reject me" (p. 108). This characterization of group behavior by Bennis and Shepard sounds very much like what would be identified in focal conflict theory as a reactive motive. Indeed, Whitaker and Lieberman's (1964) focal conflict theory adds perspective here because it gives insight into the shared conscious and unconscious group member themes and disturbing motives in terms of the secret hope for never-ending group happiness and the lurking reactive motive that someone in the group will burst the fantasy bubble which then leaves one utterly bereft (see Appendix C).

Reflecting on How You Deal With Emotional Intensity, Intimacy, and Closeness

In light of the challenges to the group related to emotional intensity and especially to closeness and intimacy concerns, the implications are that you remain alert and especially observant. You will increase your possibilities for effectiveness by action, attention to developments in the group, and thoughtful personal awareness. Again, I encourage you to listen to themes and stories and to notice where, when, and how group members build their disclosures or stories as they connect to those earlier shared by other members. Look for opportunities to notice stories of others that in some way provide you with insight into your own life stories or new ways of looking at your experiences. Also recognize that these themes and stories may provide clues about where the shared consciousness and concerns of the group and also its potential lie.

It will also be helpful to notice where you are in the closeness-intimacy mix. Also notice how the group attempts to deal with holding itself together as a unit even though in this stage, it is "shape-shifting" even as we speak. However, in spite of the possible emergence of new subfactions, notice that members deal with challenges of intimacy and closeness regardless of the subfaction or orientation to which they are inclined. This challenge affects them somehow, whether in emotional terms, psychological terms, or both. It will also be helpful to see where you are in the context of the group and see what your contributions are as a member in terms of the extent to which you involve yourself or not.

As you see the group making effort to become more self-directing, notice where you are along the dependency/nondependency continuum. Although the group leader possibly may be less active in this stage, utilize your observation skills to notice from where and from whom leadership comes to the group. In other words, notice whether or not you see yourself as someone who possesses the capacity to guide yourself. Will you take benefit somehow from the climate that presently prevails in the group? Consider what might make it advantageous for you to think in this way.

LATE MIDDLE STAGE MEMBER CHALLENGES: MORE GOOD THINGS FOR YOU TO NOTICE

Major challenges to members in the late middle stage include continued alertness, particularly in terms of themes and stories in the group. It is also an important challenge for group members to remain alert to episodes in the group that cause them to feel more connected to other members and that also bond them more tightly to each other. It will continue to be helpful to notice themes and stories, and as members become more transparent in their interactions, notice whether you fit into their stories or not. What is your sense of readiness for allowing more emotional and psychological accessibility in ways you have not been available until now? Now is a good time for group members to make another assessment of their own personal honesty in the group. It will be helpful to recognize, if they have not already, that members have the ability to notice themselves and monitor their own thoughts, feelings, behaviors, and reactions. It may be helpful for members to understand that they can help themselves and the group by modeling and exemplifying effective member behavior.

Notice what you know or do not know about yourself regarding closeness and intimacy. Notice with whom you are close or whom you are not in the group. With whom do you want to seek more friendship or emotional closeness? What do you understand about similarities and differences between emotional intimacy and sexual intimacy? Notice any fears of miscommunication or misunderstanding you may have regarding intimacy with others in the group or in your life. Notice whether you see pieces of your history coming up at this time in the group. Do you notice buried "stuff," perhaps? Do you see family hurts or pain that is yet unresolved from a relationship in the past or present?

LATE MIDDLE STAGE SCENARIOS

Late Middle Stage Scenario 8

In Session 8, Chris tells the group that she is considering looking into individual counseling. She says that she recognizes that she has unresolved traumatic issues that have led her to be highly needy, insecure, and constantly fearful that she will be emotionally abandoned. She also tells the group that she has mostly dealt with the painful things in her life by hiding and trying to behave as if everything was okay. But she also says that whenever she has come into a relationship in which she feels the possibility of a genuine emotional connection, all of what she calls her "craziness" also comes forth. When asked about her use of the word *craziness* she says she now understands it to be emotional baggage from her relationship with her father and the death of her sister Katie, with whom she felt a sense of true security and love. Before she came to understand herself in this way, she only saw her craziness as a monstrous black cloud that enveloped anyone and anything that made her happy.

Then Ria speaks up and says, "When Tony and I were in the café, we told each other some of the first impressions we had of each other in the group. We decided to do that because it wouldn't involve talking about any of you behind your backs. So Tony suggested that we tell you guys our first impressions and maybe we can get more feedback. If other folks want to talk about first impressions, maybe we can do that too."

José speaks up and says, "Talking about first impressions really sounds interesting but in some ways ... and I know I'm sounding a bit like Rick, but I think it's just a little off target. How about if people really want to talk about impressions, we make it *now* impressions and so long as people don't go overboard with 'then and there' stuff, they can add in some first impressions."

Rick raises his eyebrows in his usual way as he surveys the group. He smiles but says no words. Jewels speaks, saying, "I like it. It scares me a little 'cause I think I already know what certain people think of me. I won't say his name but his initials are José Banderas. But I would like to hear more feedback." José says, "And what impression do you think I have of you, Jewels? My inquiring mind wants to know."

"Well, we never talked that much but I always thought we had a connection," Jewels says. "It was kinda like a propinquity thing." José screws his face up and says "Pro pink what?"

> I mean I felt a connection just because of nearness. We usually sat next to each other in the group. But then you said in a joking way, which I took as serious, that you saw Doreen and me as expecting a lot from Rick. Then, you jumped into the discussion, Bill, and took it to a whole new level saying that me and Doreen were busted (caught, discovered) because the way you saw us was like we looked at Rick like we needed him to tell us whether or not to breathe. And you thought we should take ownership of that.

Bill smiles sheepishly and says, "A lot of water has gone under the bridge since I said that, but you got my words down like a court reporter, Doreen. All I can say is you're right and I am busted." Doreen says, "Well, right Bill. You're busted but you're not off the hook, 'cause I want to know how do you see me now?" Bill smiles again and sighs. "Dang," he says.

> I sure don't see you depending on Rick like I thought you did at first. I see you as a real role model in the group. Even when we started, you were the first person to speak up and even though it was in the last minute of the session. Then you faded away for a while but lately you have been blowing me away. I see you as really honest, a good listener, and a follow-up and follow-through girl 'cause when Chris gave you a hint, you jumped right on it and you came back to the group with the scoop from your father. I also have to mention that the whole way you dealt with that really started to open some doors for me in dealing with my own baggage. You see what I'm trying to say?

Doreen says, "Wow, I do! I get you clear as a bell, Bill. And I really appreciate your feedback."

Jewels, Chris, and Ria follow Bill with additional feedback to Doreen, all of them agreeing with Bill's perceptions, for the most part. Interestingly, each of the three women says how she identifies with a different person in Doreen's story. Chris for example, identifies with Doreen's estranged brother, Luke, though she gives no details. Jewels identifies with Doreen's mother, Becky, and Ria identifies with Celeste, mother of Doreen's biracial brother. Other group members find these reactions provocative and stimulating and they see, perhaps more clearly than before, how much potential and richness there is in here and now sharing. They see as well how the past can be illuminated by connecting it to the present rather than leaving it as important but nonetheless "then and there" historical review.

Chris speaks up during a pause and says, "I'm interested in two things right now. I'd really like to hear more from Jewels and Ria about how you relate to Becky and Celeste in Doreen's family. The second thing is I'd like to receive feedback from the group about how you see me now." José speaks up instantly. "Chris, I see you as one of the most supportive members of the group. If there's anybody here who can stretch their dollar, so to speak, I'd say it's you." Chris hunches her shoulders with a quizzical look on her face and says, "Uh … stretch their dollar? I guess you're referring to me but I'm not sure what you mean. If you don't mind, please explain." José says,

> What I mean is, you say few words. Sometimes you only do gestures, like you handed Bill a bottle of water. You suggested to Doreen to talk to her father. And these things which sometimes look small get big responses. I mean they seem to get payoffs for Bill and especially Doreen. So I see you as a real low-key facilitator. But you are also mysterious. You don't tell much about yourself. What you shared last session was amazing.

Tony and Jewels agree with José but Doreen jumps in to speak up for Chris. "Actions speak louder than words," she says. "And I think I'm getting to know a lot about you, Chris, by what I see you do."

Chris appears to be affected by both José's and Doreen's words. José's words seem direct and clear enough, but there is some tension that is evident. By the time he finishes saying what he has to say, Doreen steps up and her comments seem to squash the tension, and Chris begins to look relieved as color comes back to her face. Then she says, "The reason I relate to your brother Luke, Doreen, is because I feel like an orphan in my family. I got cut off from my extended family and for a long time I felt cut off from my sense of hope. I would like for you, José, and others to get to know me better, but this is as much as I can say for now." José fades into the background. Tony and Bill tell Chris that they appreciate what she does for the group. Chris says,

> I can also say in all honesty that I want you to get to know me but I have to say to you, José, that I'm finding out that I can not only be mysterious to other people. I can be a mystery to myself. I discover things in this group, I really never knew before about myself, even when it is right before my eyes sometimes.

José slumps further down into his chair. He looks at Chris and slings a sarcastic sentence: "Chris, you may be a mystery to yourself and maybe to some other people but you are not a mystery to me." Tony immediately springs to Chris's defense. Others are ready to join him. "Whoo-aa, Nelly!" Tony yells. "Whatever horse you're riding on, José, it seems to be getting away from you, man. You're eating folks alive tonight. Is something eating at you or is this your play to get out of receiving feedback? I hope not because I definitely have a bunch of it for you." José seems to fume for almost a full 60 seconds. Then he says to Tony, "You're right. I'm over the top and I'm out of line. My apologies to you, Chris, and to you, Bill." José then resumes his slumping and says nothing further for the rest of the session. The group continues without pursuing anything from him. Tony's response to José puts him back into the spotlight. He makes an attempt to escape it, but that is impossible. Several members want to interact with him, the first of them being Ria. "I'd like to know how you see me now in the group," she says.

> But I also want to give you some feedback. I see you as someone really worth looking up to. I see you kind of like a cross between an uncle and the older brother I never had. I know there are about ten or twelve years difference in our ages, but what I appreciate about you is that I never have any sense of you looking down at me. You really seem to care about others. Like in the way you just stood up for Chris and Bill. I've seen you do that for others in our group too. I think you are one of the most compassionate, fully alive men I have ever met. To me you are a real beautiful example of a good person, a hero and a warrior like your father obviously was too. When you first told us your view of the planet and pain, I thought for all the vagueness of your words, they were passionate and from the heart. It was then and is now clear to see that you've survived a lot of suffering.

Before Tony can reply, Jewels, Doreen, and Chris follow Ria with more feedback. Each of them affirms Ria's comments and adds more about how she feels in some personal way. The group has a moment of shared laughter when Jewels tells about a dream she had the first night Tony spoke in the group and said: "This planet we live on is nothing but a freakin' *Titanic*. Know what I mean?" Jewels says that as a child she used to spend time with her grandmother, a prim and proper senior lady who was very finicky about her outfits and personal appearance. She was also hard of hearing. Whenever she and Jewels spent time together, she would ask Jewels about what she was learning in school. In the dream, Jewels was with her grandmother, who asks what she learned that day and Jewels says, "Gramma, do you know that some people see the world like a sinking ship?" Gramma begins patting her hips and legs while frantically looking around to her sides and over her shoulders as if she is trying to see something behind her that moves out of sight as she turns. Young Jewels becomes worried about her gramma, who is turning herself around in the middle of the floor. "What's the matter, Gramma? Are you okay?" the child asks. Gramma answers but still with a frantic look on her face, she says, "Child, its time for us to to go out to lunch and I thought you just told me that I look like a girl with a shrinking slip." Everyone has a good laugh and Rick says, "It's been quite a session tonight. Hopefully, we'll go even further next time. Take care, everybody. See you next time."

Late Middle Stage: Group Session Schedule Update

According to the schedule for meetings handed out by Rick at the first group meeting, guidelines were also given for attendance and absences. Members who agreed to attend but who later decided to leave would inform the group of their intention to do so in person. Rick had also mentioned that Session 10 would be postponed due to a legal holiday on which the campus would be closed. This was also in the printed schedule, which everyone received. This meant that two weeks would pass before the beginning of Session 11, the actual 10th session of the group.

Early Middle Stage Challenges: Scenario 9

As Session 9 begins, the mood is light but members seem to have a hard time getting to work. The startup chatter goes on longer than the usual five minutes or so. Finally, Ria says, "Obviously, the group is in flight." José, who has resumed his slumped posture says, "Obviously, *you* must be in flight, Ria. You can't speak for the whole group and you can't speak for me." Tony springs forward and says,

> Obviously, something is bugging you, José. Unless the guy you first showed us in the early weeks of the group was counterfeit. You've been different and I wish you'd tell me and tell the group what's happening with you. Is your change of mood connected with something inside or outside of this group?

José answers, "It's really a bit of both. I'm going to just cut to the chase for everybody though. Believe it or not, I have my own 'issues' but I'm not comfortable about putting them out in this group. Also, I thought this was supposed to be a personal growth group not psychoanalysis." Rick looks up and calmly says,

> You are free to choose like everyone else here, José. No one is going to try to force you. So thanks for saying as much as you've said. On another front, it seems like the group is having a hard time getting started tonight. A lot of good things happened before. I believe good things can still happen now. So let me just say this and I'll leave each of you to decide where we go from here. If anyone wonders what is happening in the group, the answer is always going to be the same for how to find out what that is. Every group member has to say to her- or himself the following sentence: "The way to get at what is happening in the group is to get to what is happening with me."

A long pause follows Rick's comment, then Ria speaks up again.

> I'd really like for everyone here to know me. I'd really like to tell you about some of my hopes and dreams. I've been so strongly affected by some of the stories that have been shared here in our group. We've touched on a lot of things that deal with families and really painful stuff like we heard from Doreen, Tony, and Chris. When I hear stories from you guys, it makes me think of my own family life. I've wanted to tell you all my story, but then I see my own monsters and horrifying fears, you know, so then I just keep hiding that part of myself 'cause I'm scared that if I tell you, you all might reject me or be hating on me and I just don't think I can take any more of that.

Doreen leaves her chair to sit closer to Ria as she continues speaking.

> See, to make a long story short, my mama gave me away. Actually, she abandoned me because she left me in a basket on the steps of the Phyllis Wheatley Community Center. I can remember many times when I had thoughts like, "Why didn't she just flush me down the toilet or throw me into a dumpster?" I know I shouldn't be thinking like this, but I grew up in a series of foster families. Did any of y'all read the book *Finding Fish*? His life was heaven compared to mine. But the thing I want to share with you all is that for most of my life, I never felt like I was worthy of being loved. I'm better now than I used to be, thanks to Ms. Jackie, a mentor I met in my senior year of high school. But I know I've still got a lot of baggage because I've been afraid that if I told you about my past, you all might want to give me away too because you think I'm not worthy of your love.

Doreen begins to weep. Soon she is sobbing. Everyone in the group physically moves toward Doreen and Ria. Doreen is patting her eyes with a tissue as she says, "That is one of the saddest sentences I have ever heard, Ria. That if I heard about your past, I might or maybe the group might want to give you away because we think you are not worthy of our love. Oh my Lord. What you are saying just breaks my heart." Doreen blows her nose then continues.

> Because you are *so* worthy in my eyes. But I'm glad you told us, 'cause in my book, you really deserve better. Oh, and I just want to say to José that I'm glad to see you sitting up in your chair. Since you went into what looks to me like a role reversal with Bill with all this slumping stuff, I've really been worried about you. But you sitting up to listen to Ria means a lot to me.

José smiles a bit and nods. Chris speaks next and says, "Well, I told you all part of my story. I guess my fear is that everyone I love will leave or will love someone else. Listening to you, Ria, really helps me see where I'm at." Tony follows Chris and says,

> Much like Chris and Doreen, I've told you folks my story but I have not told you my secret horrifying fear—as Ria dubbed hers. I've been deeply touched, too, by what everyone has shared here and amazed at where our group has gone. What I haven't told you, that Chris helped make clear for me, is that my fear is not only that everyone I love will leave me but also that they will die. That is why this planet is like a freakin' *Titanic* for me. Everyone I have ever loved when I was growing up died. My mother. My father and my grandmother. For a long time, secretly I thought I was the reason they died. I never thought I'd be talking about these things in this group. But when I got here and sat down in our circle, my pain just came bubbling up to the surface. That impossible question also came bubbling up and when I heard myself saying it to all of you, I could hardly believe myself."

Another silence falls on the group as members seemed to collectively hover in the feeling of closeness and understanding. Bill speaks up and says,

> In this moment, I'm feeling hopeful. I didn't think anybody could understand how doggone wretched my pain is. I thought I was alone and I am amazed by what has been shared here. I want to tell you all more of my story. See, I've been in a state of panic since Ria and Tony mentioned us possibly sharing group member secrets. For me, the mere mention of the word *secret* changes my heart rate and makes it harder for me to breathe. The reason the word secret bothers me so much is because when I was a kid, maybe age four or almost five, my parents were on the verge of divorce because my mother was having an affair. When my dad discovered it was happening, he went berserk. He was a monster masquerading as a nice guy, but still he loved my mother a lot. My dad is Brazilian and my mother is French American. They had only two children, my older sister Nicole and me. When my mother told my father about her affair, he left and after this my mom began to drink. My father wanted my sister and me to live with him but my mother didn't want that to happen. So she made a plan to stop my dad from getting us. My mother's plan almost caused my father to commit murder and it estranged us all forever. My mother told my father that neither my sister nor I were his children. My mother also told me that she was going to tell me a secret. I was hardly five when this happened. She told me that my real father was my uncle, my father's brother. But she told my sister, she was ten at the time, that her secret was really a lie. When I saw my father at Christmas, I innocently asked him how Uncle Paulo could be my dad. My father asked me why I thought this and I told him that Mommy told me but it's a secret so please don't tell. And my dad went crazy and beat his brother and threatened to shoot my mother. Finally, she moved with us to another city and our dad was restrained. But the more I grew and learned about what a secret meant, the sadder and sadder I got.

Bill became choked up now and then as he told his story and a few members were moved to tears. But José was not among them. He sat with his hands to his head, his elbow on his knees as he stared at the floor in silence. Without looking up he says, "What I wonder is whether or not you and your sister were born of incest or not."

Every single member of the group springs to his or her feet and Bill has already sprung toward José with both arms extended, his hands like claws aimed for José's neck. Had Tony not grabbed Bill and restrained him, a fight would likely have happened in the group. Group members jeered at José as Rick escorted him to a far corner of the room to talk to him. Members were saying things like, "No he didn't! You need to take that back, José right this minute! You went too far this time." Then Tony says, "You're really acting like a freakin' jerk, man. What the hell are you trying to prove?" Then Doreen says, "If this is a preview of the kind of psychology you're going to practice, heaven help your clients." While the group is challenging José and attempting to calm Bill down, Chris flees the room weeping. Rick notices and asks Ria to go after her. Ria pursues her all the way outside to the parking lot, but Chris reaches her car and speeds away as Ria stands helpless in the fumes. When Ria returns to the group, the group has reconvened and Bill and José are standing behind their chairs on opposite sides of the room. Rick has taken a very strong position in the group about safety and asks everyone to stay for 15 minutes longer to attempt some kind of resolution. He insists that José cannot leave the room until making an apology that Bill can hear and possibly accept. José looks remorseful and Bill is beginning to calm down. José says "I was way out of line, Bill. I'm sorry and I hope we can work it out. I see I've got issues that don't have anything to do with you. I apologize, man, sincerely." Bill listens and observes José through his explanation then he says,

> You've come at me before, José but *this time* you've completely violated my trust, and left me completely amazed that I ever believed you were a good man. I am embarrassed at how much I permitted your words to penetrate into my heart. I really wanted to hurt you tonight. I cannot accept your apology in this moment but I will think long and hard about everything I've heard from you tonight. Maybe it's good that we're not meeting next week. But I want everyone in this group to know that I will not let anyone drive me away from this group." Rick expresses his appreciation to José and Bill and to the group members for their patience and support. "I thank you all. I hope to see everyone again after the break.

Everyone leaves the room in silence. It seems that José leaves the room in utter embarrassment. Bill and a few others depart in anger or in shock, and some depart with a sense of complete helplessness and confusion as to what has just happened in the group tonight.

Early Middle Stage: Scenario 11

It is very obvious that a member is missing at the beginning of Session 11. Chris's empty chair leaves a gaping hole in the circle that is immediately noticed and felt by the group. Surprisingly, José is present. He is silent and sitting forward, staring at the floor. Rick looks around the group. After a long silence he says,

> If anyone regrets missing the group because of the holiday, you are not alone. The break came at the worst time. The days passed more slowly than chilled molasses and I regret that we did not convene last week. But such things do happen in the life of groups. It may have been for the best. I'm very happy to see almost everyone here tonight. Chris is obviously not with us. I have heard nothing from her since the last time we were here. Ria saw her drive away from the parking lot. The group must decide where it will go from here.

Tony's lips are pursed and the tension lines along his jawbone are clear to see. Doreen and Ria notice, but Doreen speaks up first. "Is something happening with you, Tony?" she says. "You're looking real tight tonight." "Yeah, something is happening with me," he answers.

> If you haven't guessed already, I'm still freakin' pissed. I've been trying to put it behind me and when I came tonight, I thought I was okay but every time I think of José's words to Bill and Chris running out of the room in tears, I get angry all over again. I am angry with myself for being so angry and I am angry with you, José, because I do not understand where you're coming from. I didn't expect you to be here tonight, but since you are, I really wish you would tell

me and tell us what made you ask Bill that question. It was easy to see that he was vulnerable and hurting.

José stands up and without looking into anyone's eyes says, "I've been debating with myself about whether to come back here or not tonight. You're right, Tony, I should go."

Ria immediately runs to the door and stands with her back to it with her arms outstretched. "You can go, José. Yeah, you can go. But when you do, you're gonna have to go through me. I'm not moving till you give me, give us, some kind of explanation. Preferably, you tell us the truth." José says, "I really want to go." Ria says, "I ain't moving one inch." Rick stands up, as does Tony, Bill, Doreen, Jewels, and you. Something about Chris's departure has affected you and because you know something about her that she has not yet disclosed to the group, you feel special empathy for her struggle. But you aren't surprised that she is not here for today's session. The tension is mounting in the room and every member feels it because this group has radar for anxiety and conflict. Rick says,

> Ria, not only am I going to ask you to step aside, I'm going to ask you to open the door wide. And José, I'm going to ask you to choose like we have not seen you do before. I am asking you to let us know the part of you that said those words to Bill and let us really be with you and hear you. Or you can choose to stuff your painful things inside wherever it is that you stuff them and you can walk out that door pretending we never existed.

Rick looks at Ria and says, "Ria, I respectfully implore you to step away from the door. And José, I ask you to choose." Everything becomes quiet in the room for at least a full minute. It is reminiscent of the very first session in the moments that followed Rick's first introductory remarks to the group. Suddenly, José sits down on the floor, exactly where he stood. He covers his face and says,

> I am so-oo sorry and so embarrassed. I was so wrong but I did not even see what I must have sounded like until after I said the words. After I got home, I kept hearing all your voices over and over saying, "No he didn't," "What are you trying to prove?" "You're acting like a jerk, man." "You went too far." "Heaven help your clients." I finally had to do some soul searching and ask myself why I've been so bothered by everything, not just Chris or Bill. It has been such an irrational bother. Actually, it is more than bother, it is masked anger. I tried not to let it show but I could not hide it. You are all probably wondering what and why? I knew nothing about Chris or Bill except what I've seen and heard in this group. But it isn't just with them. I have been on the edge a lot lately. I was over the top with you, Ria and others, not even to mention Bill. But I have been trying to hide it. In the past, I was better at it.

José heaves a big sigh and continues.

> Part of what is happening with me is that I lost a girl I loved almost three years ago about this time of year. Every year about this time, I'm angry without knowing why and then I remember or realize what month it is. Her name is

Leanne but everybody called her LeeLee. Well, she actually dumped me—and here's where Bill comes in. LeeLee dumped me for a guy who was supposed to be my friend and believe it or not, he was a Brazilian guy whose name was Paulo, too. Well, LeeLee married him. And why did she marry Paulo? She married Paulo because José did not know how to treat her. He did not know how to talk honestly. If he felt vulnerable he was sarcastic, sometimes he was unjustifiably caustic. If he was confronted, somebody or something else was always the problem and one day, LeeLee had enough. Even Paulo eventually had enough and I began to see less and less of him. Several months after LeeLee and I broke up, she ran into Paulo. They felt a spark and the rest is history after that. So Bill, when you mentioned that your father was Brazilian and that his name is also Paulo, I just went on automatic in my negative association and I tried to hurt you with my question. I often did the same with LeeLee. How sick is that, right? I think I need personal counseling way more than Chris. I don't see how I can possibly stay in this group. In this moment, I feel like cow dung is actually more worthy than me. A Mexican man hating a Brazilian when really it is himself he hates. The Brazilian man did nothing. I know that you're not Paulo, Bill. I even know that Paulo is not the problem. I know that my anger toward him and others is my projection and my own self-hatred, which is not on my radar most of the time. But now you all are forcing me not only to face how ugly it is but also to face my own self-created pain. And right now, José the psychology major feels more shame than he has ever felt before. I'm really sorry for my behavior too.

Then Ria pipes up and says, "Sorry. Sorry? Hmph. You apologized to Bill and it sounds like now you're apologizing to us but you need to apologize to Chris." José sighs deeply and says, "Maybe you are right, Ria—and that's another thing I'm so jealous of you about, cause most of the time you are right and you seem to do the right thing most of the time in this group. But my psychology background has not taken me that far."

"So now you're gonna blame your problems on your psychology major?" Ria says. "Touché, Ria. I guess you are right yet again," says José. Then Tony speaks up and says, "It's really hard for me to see how we can go ahead in this group. It feels like the hole is just too big. Man, I'm so glad I didn't leave. And Bill, I'm so glad you didn't leave. Now I can see what it might have been like for others if I had chosen to check out of the group."

Doreen speaks up and says,

> Checkout really resonates with how I'm feeling right now. I had a real hard time coming back tonight. I was flying so high in this group. You guys supported me through some major stuff. I trusted all of you. Even though you always challenged me, José, I trusted you too. But it seems like you've gone into a real Dr. Jekyll–Mr. Hyde modus operandi and I don't really know who you are. I almost want to lash out at you like you did at Bill and say something like is the story you just told us really true or do you just want to manipulate your way off the hook?

Then Jewels says, "My contributions have been limited here. I never set the group on fire but I see my life experience is limited too. I have learned so much from all of you, but I really miss Chris. And José, I'm glad you stayed and I'm asking you to please help me to regain my faith in you."

You are silent again for large portions of this session, but you are struck by Doreen's and Jewels' remarks. You initiate giving them both feedback that tells how you have seen them grow immensely in the group. You tell Doreen that you see her as courageous in her honesty, not only in terms of what she shares but also in how she risks of herself in what she says to others. You tell her that her words tonight to José are a recent example. You then say one sentence to José: "I just want to find that the things you've shared tonight are the real true you."

Early Middle Stage Scenario 11: Alternative Ending A

Ria then says, "I'd like to do one more thing before we close. I'd like to call Chris on her cell phone. If I do, José, will you speak to her?" José says, "If she'd even give me the time of day, I'd be grateful." So Ria calls. As she punches the numbers, she says to the group, "We just exchanged numbers last session before the break at the vending machines before group got started." Ria pauses as the phone rings. She says, "Hello, Chris? Hi. It's Ria. How are you? Or should I not ask? Girl, I'm calling you from our group because things are not right without you in it. I'm going to put someone on. Please don't hang up, okay? Alright, just a sec." Ria hands the phone over to José. He says,

> Hello Chris, please don't hang up. This is José. I know the words I said were hurtful. The regret I feel is more than I can put into words. I'm so sorry and I have apologized to Bill and to the group. I'm really so sorry and I've been a mess for the past two weeks. I made some conscious and unconscious decisions about Bill without any real basis. No … no. Please hear me out. No, I'm the problem. I have a problem. I don't believe that Bill is the problem and if I ever sounded like he was the problem, then my perception was simply screwed up. Look Chris, I need you here to talk about this more. In brief, I have bad history with a Brazilian person, so I projected my anger and my issues onto Bill's Brazilian heritage. There is more but for now, just let me say that I finally made a choice to share my story, but I've been such a jerk and so inconsistent, some people don't believe me or trust anything I say. I wouldn't blame you if you felt the same. I just want to say that you are so needed in this group. There's a gaping hole without you. Please, I ask you to please consider coming back. Alright, now I'm going to put Ria on again, okay?

Ria takes the phone and as she says "Hi," all the group members give a shout out to Chris saying, "We all miss you, Chris. Please come back. You're our buried treasure, Chris. Please come back to our group."

Early Middle Stage Scenario 11: Alternative Ending: B

Ria then says, "I'd like to do one more thing before we close. I'd like to call Chris on her cell phone. If I do, José, will you speak to her?" José says, "If she'd even give me the time of day, I'd be grateful." So Ria calls. As she punches the numbers, she says to the group, "We just exchanged numbers last session before the break at the vending machines before group got started." Ria pauses as the phone rings. She says,

"Hello, Chris? Hi. It's Ria. How are you? Or should I not ask? Girl, I'm calling you from our group because things are not right without you in it. I'm going to put someone one. Please don't hang up, okay? Alright, just a sec." Ria hands the phone over to José. He says, "Hello Chris, please don't hang up." There is a long pause, then the call disconnects. José looks stunned. "She didn't even say hello," José says, not looking in any ascertainable direction.

> She was quiet for a long time and then she just hung up. Now I'm feeling really guilty. I know I'm not that great a group member, but right now I'm feeling very inadequate, like I can't do anything right in this group lately. I know it's entirely my own fault, but that doesn't necessarily make it any better.

Momentarily, to everyone's sheer amazement, Chris shows up at the door. Her open cell phone is still in her hand and she appears to be very tired. Everyone in the room cheers. Then Ria welcomes her saying, "Come on over her girlfriend. I'm really glad you're back, or here—whatever." Chris walks toward her chair in the circle. She tells the group how she has agonized about having left the group without giving anyone an explanation. But she also says she had to do it. Moreover, she says,

> I sped out of the parking lot, leaving Ria standing there when I knew she had come to help me. How stupid and selfish of me. She was my best connection to the group but I didn't give her a chance. I know that the group is almost out of time tonight. I just wanted to let all of you know that I want to be here. And I want you to know, José, that your comments to Bill upset me a lot. By the way, how are you Bill? While I was out, I wondered if you felt like running away too. You're a strong man, Bill, stronger than you seem. I wish I had your strength. José I want to say to you that it's not just what you said but something about *how* you said it. It sounded harsh and mean-spirited. I felt hurt, as if you'd said the words to me. That's part of my problem, because you reminded me of my baggage. Somehow that whole episode last week tapped into some old painful stuff … family stuff. So tonight, when I heard your voice, I just froze. I almost ran away again, but I knew that I couldn't do that. I had already told myself that I'd come to the group and talk to all of you tonight. I was just passing the vending machines again when you called me, Ria. But when you put José on, I freaked. I almost ran off again but finally I chose not to do that again.

Then Rick said, "On behalf of the group, I welcome you back, Chris. Several members have acknowledged what a great hole in the group is left by your absence. I'm glad you came tonight. Hopefully, we'll all be here together next time."

Multicultural Considerations: Late Middle Stage

Early in Session 8, Chris discloses to the group that she is considering individual counseling. She reveals that she has seen how her unresolved traumatic concerns have been a key influence in her feelings of neediness, insecurity, and constant fearfulness that she will be emotionally abandoned. From the perspective of Bowman's (1996) multicultural training, Chris's disclosure is ripe with meaning because it demonstrates her growing self-awareness and insight into her own intrapsychic (personal) processes. Chris's insight also shows that perhaps unaware to her, she has formed emotional connections that led her to recognize how her defensive reactions that emerge when high emotions are prevalent have recently "clicked-in" and become apparent to her in the group. Chris tells her fellow group members how her usual strategy for dealing with painful things in her life is hiding, denial, and behaving as if everything is okay. She also shares that the emergence of what she refers to as her own craziness occurs only at those times when she feels that a genuine emotional connection may be possible. When group members inquire into further meanings of her self-described crazy behavior, Chris further shares that she understands it to be emotional baggage from her relationship with her father and the loss of her sister, Katie, with whom she felt a true sense of security and love. Chris also discloses that she saw the craziness "as a monstrous cloud that enveloped anyone and anything that made me happy." Chris also sees how her happiness and potentially supportive relationships are sabotaged by her craziness in the form of the enveloping monstrous cloud. The "ripeness" of Chris's opportunity is also connected to the setting in which she comes to her discovery. Bowman's discussion of the importance of experiential training and direct contact with culturally different peoples suggests that because Chris's discoveries are occurring inside a group that is culturally, socially, and racially diverse, she has an opportunity to move from knowing that cultural differences exist to knowing how to interact effectively and with self-confidence in relationships with people who are culturally different from herself.

In many ways, this type of discovery-learning as suggested by Bowman (1996) is highly prevalent in Session 8. Several members, including Ria, Tony, Jewels, José, Bill, and Doreen, actively solicit feedback and open themselves to the possibility of learning about themselves through perceptions of others about how they relate. Further, Doreen's following up on Chris's encouragement to talk to her father leads to even more disclosure in the group by Doreen. Additionally, Doreen's disclosures about her biracial brother are found to be provocative and stimulating to other members who see the power of sharing in the here and now. Doreen also gains insight into how others relate to her and how they are affected by her story. Doreen's perspective is broadened even more when Jewels reveals how much she identifies with Doreen's mother, Becky. Then Ria discloses how she identifies with the father's partner, Celeste, the mother of Doreen's biracial brother. As Session 8 unfolds, the group experiences a great deal of interpersonal disclosure and exchanges of feedback. Group members also experience a great deal of learning, discovery, and insight at individual, group, and recapitulated family levels.

José's sarcasm, which leads to his being challenged by Tony, is relevant in multicultural terms. The interaction between the two men leads to more potential cross-cultural insight. It also provokes much unsolicited feedback from group members to José. Tony's challenge to José leads to feedback from Ria about her perceptions of Tony. She shares her views about him as a person in relationship to his family and to his father in particular. Jewel's story of her interaction with her grandmother fosters comic relief from the tension between José and Tony and the earlier seriousness of Chris's and Doreen's disclosures.

At the start of Session 9, the group is in flight. José's critical and aloof-seeming observation of what is already apparent provokes reactions from several group members, including Rick, the leader. Rick's reminder to the group that the way of getting to what it is that keeps the group stuck in certain times is to get to what is happening with oneself shows the power of Bowman's (1996) strategies for multicultural learning and development through self-awareness.

Ria's disclosure, which follows a long pause in the group after Rick's comment, emotionally rocks the group and touches several members. Ria's openness leads to other significant, sometimes even "risky," disclosures from members that finally foster a group-wide sense of interpersonal connection across what may have earlier seemed secretly held and culturally fostered ideas of ethnicity, color, and race. On the heels of Ria's disclosure, while the group is still completely filled with a sense of closeness and understanding, Bill ventures forth to share his pain and his amazing story about his mother's infidelity and her false and brutal method of persuading his father that their children were not his. José responds to the story shared by Bill with a question that enrages the entire group. Chris flees the room weeping. From the perspective of self-awareness, José appears to be completely out of touch with his demeanor, words, and impact on Bill and the other members of the group. Session 10 ends on a sad, heavy, and confusing note. Most members leave in silence, completely stunned by the turn of events involving Bill, José, and Chris.

When the group reconvenes for Session 11, Chris's empty chair is noticeable to everyone. Much to the surprise of most group members, José returns that night. Rick assumes leadership and speaks directly to Chris's apparent absence. When Doreen notices that Tony appears to be very quiet and tense, she asks him what is happening and he says that he is still angry with José. Tony also says that every time he thinks of what José said to Bill followed by Chris's running out of the room in tears, he gets angry all over again. Then he gets angry at himself for being so angry. Tony asks José why he would ask Bill such a question as he had asked when anyone could easily have seen that Bill was already exposed and deep in pain. José says that he wants to go, but Ria immediately runs to the door and blocks it as she stands with her arms outstretched. She demands that José not leave before giving her and the group an explanation. Rick, Tony, Bill, Jewels, and Youtu all stand up, anticipating conflict.

Rick intervenes and asks Ria to step aside and open the door. He also asks José to choose by honestly disclosing what made him say the words he said to Bill or, alternatively, stuffing the feelings and leaving as if the group never existed. José considers his choice. Finally, José acknowledges his denial and misplaced sarcasm, which had been a cover for his guilt. In José's mind, his harshness toward Bill was justified by the fact that Bill was half Brazilian. Now José is beginning to see his behavior and his prejudice in clear perspective and he does not like what he sees. In some ways, the intrapsychic issues he was deciding to face were equally as powerful as the diversity and cultural issues that were also prevalent in the interactions.

From the point of view of Bowman's (1996) learning about oneself and how one relates to others, José faces his self-created pain and shame and apologizes to the group for his behavior toward Bill and the group. Ria speaks up to say that even though José had apologized to Bill and the group, she thought he still needed to apologize to Chris. José seizes the opportunity of the moment to tell Ria how much he admires but also envies her intuitive hunches about what to do. It seems to him that she always knows the right thing to do and that, in his opinion, she makes facilitative choices most of the time.

Several other group members make initiatives after José. Doreen follows Ria, then Jewels makes a self-assessment of her own contributions. She also expresses how much she has learned from other group members and says that she misses Chris. Finally, Jewels says to José that she is glad he stayed but also shares that she has lost faith in him and needs his help to restore it. Youtu, who has often been silent during this session, comes forward to express being struck by Doreen and Jewel's comments. Youtu tells Doreen that she or he perceives Doreen as courageous in her honesty and risk-taking and concludes with one comment to José, namely: "I just want to find that the things you've shared tonight are the real true you."

In both alternate endings for Scenario 11, Ria asks for one final activity before the group closes. She suggests calling Chris on her cell phone and asks José if he would speak to Chris. In each case, José agrees and hopes that Chris will talk to him. In the first instance, Chris doesn't hang up and José expresses his regret and tells her about his apologies to Bill and the group. He explains a little about his internal processes in terms of how he had projected his anger onto Bill's Brazilian heritage and also admits to being so inconsistent that people don't believe or trust what he says. Much to Chris's surprise, José acknowledges that there is a gaping hole in the group without her and asks her to come back. In fact, the group members shout to Chris that they all miss her and they ask if she'll come back.

In the second instance, again Ria asks to do one last thing before closing and suggests calling Chris. She asks José if he will speak to her and he agrees. Ria puts José on the phone and asks Chris not to hang up. Ria then hands the phone over to José. After he says hello, there is a long pause followed by the click of a disconnection. José is stunned, but not really. He tells the group that Chris didn't even say hello. José tells group members that he feels guilty, inadequate, and unable to do anything right in the group. But to the surprise of everyone, within minutes Chris shows up at the door of the group room. Everyone is amazed, but she is welcomed with cheers. As she moves toward her chair in the circle, Chris tells everyone how much she agonized about having left the group without giving any explanation. Chris tells group members that she wants to be in the group. She asks Bill how he is. She tells him that she wondered if he felt like running away. She also tells him that she sees him as a strong man and that she wishes she had his strength. She tells José how mean and harsh his words sounded to her. She goes on to tell him how hurt she felt, as if the words had been said to her. Then Chris glances directly into José's eyes and says: "That is part of my problem, because you reminded me of my baggage. Somehow, that whole episode last week tapped into some old painful stuff." Chris tells everyone she simply "freaked out" when she reached the vending machines. When she heard José's voice she wanted to keep on running but somehow she chose not to do that again.

Looking at Scenario 11 and its alternate endings from the perspective of multicultural considerations and Bowman's (1996) model yields several interesting ideas. Ria, who is a young African American woman, has consistently shown leadership in the group. She emerges again when she physically blocks José, a Mexican American man who has been caustic in his verbal responses and sarcastic reactions to group developments. Ria's interactions with men have shown her to be self-confident, spontaneous, compassionate, and powerful. She has demonstrated these qualities to such an extent that she has made group members see her as a unique person in the group who can stand as a significant force. She is a role model for other women in the group and perhaps at last for José, who may have personal, cultural, or gender-based biases that interfere with his ability to relate to women in particular and more generally to both men and women.

The group does not explore underlying cultural dynamics to a great degree, but there is a great deal of self-discovery, self-awareness, and developing insight in terms of how members relate to each other. This insight helps them to see how they can assist each other to make the group a fertile environment for more challenging, provocative topics that move more deeply into family and ethnicity, as well as cultural and racial aspects of gender relations in groups and other social settings. Clearly, José's shift from being closed and retreating to such a degree that he was once ready to leave the group to a posture of more self-disclosing transparency is significant. Also, Chris's emotional reaction and insights gained into her own historical emotional subterranean remnants and trauma are valuable. It is clear that a meaningful level of interpersonal learning was fostered in this group by the self-initiated disclosures from members over the course of the session. In some ways, the group cheering for Chris is emblematic of a group cheer for itself. The group has maintained itself as a productive working unit and prevailed in the face of formidable challenges aimed at causing its fragmentation and falling apart.

QUESTIONS FOR CHAPTER REVIEW

1. What are your reactions to this session?
2. What themes are most prevalent in this session?
3. Which members and which disclosures affected you most?
4. Why do you think the group had difficulty getting started in this session?
5. What are your reactions to José?
6. Youtu was relatively silent in this group. If she or he were able to take a more active role than you did, what might she or he say or do?
7. What are your reactions to Ria's use of her cell phone?
8. Where is the leadership in the group at this time?

PART 1 PROLOGUE TIPS FOR THE LATE MIDDLE STAGE

Key Components of an Effective Member Mindset

Keep in Mind the Interactive Process of Group Work

- Throughout the life of the group it is important that you actively attempt to observe what happens between yourself and other members.

- It is helpful to notice what happens between you and the group leader, what happens between you and the group, and what happens between you within the context of the group as a unit or system.
- The issue confronted by the group at any particular time denotes the group's stage of development.
- An effective group member notices which issues and related themes are most prevalent in the group interaction.

Learn How to Think in Process Terms and Distinguish Between Content and Process

- Your answers to the question, "What is happening in the group?" will likely identify something related to content.
- Your answers to the questions, "How are things happening in this group?" and "What is the feeling/tone that accompanies 'the what'?" will likely identify something related to process.

Develop the Capacity to Handle Conflict and Confrontation

- Conflict may be intrapersonal, meaning that it is internal to yourself, or interpersonal, which means that it is between you and one or more other people.
- Experiential learning settings encourage interpersonal contact that immediately forces members into greater awareness of their boundaries. For this reason, conflict in groups may happen simultaneously on more than one level.

Cultivate Conditions Within That Foster Growth in Yourself and Others

- An effective group participant is always seeking balance between his or her own inner-focused development and relationships with others in the group.
- A facilitative, growth engendering attitude reflects three qualities. Namely, these are congruence, empathy, and unconditional positive regard (Rogers, 1961).
- When working to establish empathy with another person, you grapple with establishing "dynamic balance" in which you are deeply involved with the other but not overinvolved and, simultaneously, you are detached but not aloof.

Choose to Become a Group-Work Apprentice

- Any apprentice who seeks mastery must qualify for entering apprenticeship by three steps: interest, openness to discovery about self and others, and willingness to change.

PART 2 PROLOGUE TIPS FOR THE LATE MIDDLE STAGE

Basic Strategies and Skills for Successful Involvement in the Group

- Be here now
- Listen and reflect
- Learn to convey and receive feedback
- Express feelings as feelings
- Monitor your personal process
- Utilize the three-lenses approach for practicing skills and staying involved
- Track your awareness, discovery, and learning by keeping a journal

4

Ending Stage (Termination)

MAJOR MEMBER CHALLENGES IN THE ENDING STAGE

The ending stage is the stage in which the group faces its inevitable demise together with the loss of the associated meaningful relationships of its members. Several authors speak to the uncertainty that group members feel as they grapple with leaving the group and moving on to social relationships beyond the group. These authors also speak to the feelings of denial, apprehension, and ambivalence that are highly prevalent in this stage where group members are challenged to deal with the conscious and unconscious impacts of imminent change (Bennis & Shepard, 1956; Corey, M.S. & Corey, G., 2006; Donigian & Malnati, 1997; Kline, 2003; Tuckman, 1965; Yalom, 1995).

The atmosphere of the group in this stage may vary widely depending on the constellation of members' personalities assembled and the extent to which members have gained insight into such things as their own personal styles of relating to others, their awareness of the impact of experiences within their early family life, especially as relate to communication, self-sharing, openness, or caution in expressing feelings. Also important are members' experiences with nurturance and their sense of having been cared for or not by caregivers. Members' sense of stability or instability in valued significant relationships is important and, finally, their sense of worth in the eyes of others and sense of confidence in their own value and potential.

CHARACTERISTICS OF THE ENDING STAGE: HELPFUL THINGS TO NOTICE

Reaching this stage of the group has implications for you in terms of the challenges you are likely to face. This includes what kinds of things you are likely to feel and what kinds of interactions you are likely to have, particularly when you enter a group where the climate I have just described prevails and you are left to discover how and where you fit into it.

Your self-awareness, your discoveries about your orientation to relationships, your understanding of how your experiences in your family have influenced your perceptions of others, and your orientation toward making contact are all fundamentally important here. Your ability to be present, that is to stay here and now will be very helpful. The main question you are faced with is: can you be in a complex, stimulating, highly emotional, and social environment and be your most honest, actively engaged self without becoming overwhelmed? The implication is that if your answer is yes, you are more likely to be effective when you approach the opening of the ending stage.

ENDING STAGE GROUP CHALLENGES: GOOD THINGS FOR YOU AS A MEMBER TO NOTICE

The major challenge to the group in the ending stage is to keep its energies and attention focused to the present. It is a natural part of the group's evolution that the members review significant past group episodes as the end of their time together in the group approaches. The finality of the end often reverberates more deeply than the group and its members expect. Sometimes, the looming prospect of ending, which brings with it related issues of loss, loneliness, isolation, and alienation, strikes deeply at subterranean feelings in unconscious realms. Memories of historical losses, separations through death, divorce, unsuccessful loves, and strained family relations may be stirred to group members' unawares.

The prevalence of blissful reminiscence is understandable and to some extent functional, in the sense that it mediates feelings related to impending change. However, the group is still faced with the essential challenge of balance, of how to look back and glance ahead without losing its grounding in the now. This is because now is the place where the group can help members see into the issues and learn from the experiences that have been provided by the group, which, if understood, can send members to social relationships beyond the group ready to participate more effectively, toward the end of greater balance, mutuality, and success.

The implications of the group challenge for you as a member at this stage of the group are that you can increase your effectiveness and your possibilities of leaving the group with skills, tools, and resources that show you the pitfalls of past failures, losses, and orientations. Some of these may even be decisions based on past family experiences. On the other hand, you can leave the group with an awareness of the greater positive possibilities of relationships and with tools in hand for preventing repeated past negative choices. You may leave with tools for creating the things you hope for in relationships with others in routine daily living, in friendships, in relationships at work, and in love, intimate, and family relationships.

Reflecting on How You Deal With Change and Transition

The major member challenge for the ending stage is to understand and grapple with the complexity of the ending stage transition. The member needs an awareness of his or her unique ways of coping with existential questions of loss and ending. As a member, you will face this challenge when it becomes clear to you that the group will end, as do many things in life. When this finality is acknowledged, then the possibility comes for next steps, even though what those steps are exactly, may in the moment seem to be unknown. Group members see that this group, which has been a cauldron of experiences, will not continue and one cannot ever reconstruct it or return to it after it ends—though there may be countless groups to explore elsewhere.

Some members may notice that experiences within their original families have provided them with tools. Things such as the loss of a first pet or the death of a family member may provide ideas for how to cope with loss or lessons of how to be alone and remain healthy. Alternatively, members may have been too wounded by their losses to take lessons. In such cases, addressing the wounds becomes the challenge here and now. Member behavior in this stage can be instructive for you as an individual because you are presented with a living experience that often parallels other groups and situations in life.

You have a great chance of taking some kind of benefit if you are interested and paying attention. You will likely see a range of coping styles in terms of how members deal with change, loss, and ending. You will also likely see how losses of the past are recapitulated and replayed in the group, sometimes to the member's great advantage. At these times a member gets a chance to revise his or her decisions about pain of the past, missed opportunities that still cause grief, or other unresolved historical issues. One gets to see some people whose solution is a simple choice to opt out. The ending is for some like a scene in a horror movie. Some people close their eyes and wait for the scary moment to pass. Some move more slowly, with the hope of delay or postponement of the inevitable.

ENDING STAGE MEMBER CHALLENGES: MORE GOOD THINGS FOR YOU TO NOTICE

The most important challenge for you in the ending stage is that you hear the words of the lesson. In other words, your personal challenge is to tune in, in order to see how others meet or miss the challenge. Your challenge is to tune in, so that you may take each person's struggle, dialogue, disclosure, and demonstrated resistance as instruction for yourself. The implication is that you might come to see a path leading out of isolation, loneliness, fear, and being stuck, not necessarily by doing anything more than being with that path, acknowledging it by saying, "I'm scared, I'm lonely, I miss you. This is what I see you do. This is what I see myself doing." These expressions of feelings and what is being experienced are also strategies in themselves for finding a way out.

ENDING STAGE SCENARIOS

Ending Stage Characteristics: Scenario 12

When Session 12 convenes, all the members are present and everyone is in the room on time. There is a slight bit of tension in the atmosphere, but members talk to each other and make lighthearted chitchat in the usual way. After about five minutes, Jewels is the first to speak. She says,

> I said to the group that I see my contributions in here as limited, but I want you all to know that I don't want to be a limited member anymore. And lately, I've felt myself really involved, with lots of feelings and gut-churning reactions to things that happen in our group. One person in this group I've felt really connected to is you, Ria, but I have been too embarrassed to tell you. Mostly because I thought you'd see me as the "little White girl" who grew up in a "little White world" who has no clue about how people from other worlds suffer and struggle to survive. You've never said it to me but if you did, you wouldn't be too far off because the house I grew up in actually had a white picket fence in an all-White neighborhood. Probably the most upsetting thing that happened to me in all my adolescent years was my mother deciding to give my ice skates away. I had outgrown them three years earlier but they had sentimental value. I cannot tell you how moved I am by your story, Ria, and what you have survived in beautiful ways. I'm not feeling as low as that cow dung José mentioned, but I am feeling very embarrassed that I have so little to complain about. I was upset that I had a mother who wanted to give my old skates away. But you had a mother who gave baby Ria away, the precious child version of who you are now today. I don't know who she was. Maybe she was a scared eighteen-year-old. I don't know who her mother was or how she was raised. I cannot judge her. But regardless of who she was, I want you to know that I believe that you so deserve to be kept, Ria. You so deserve it, and I am so proud and honored to know you. So I wanted to say these things to you. I hope I can be your friend, Ria. Why anyone who has you in their life now would want to give you away, I cannot even imagine.

Ria interjects, "I don't mean to cut you off but I have to say two things. First, I don't see you as a color, Jewels. I notice your color, but I don't judge you only by that. See, the best foster mother I ever had—the only mother I've ever known—is White. And number two—you *are* my friend."

Jewel's eyes well up with tears. After a moment she continues her feedback,

> I also want to say to you, José, that I'm stunned by your behavior in the group. Your apology to Bill sounded heartfelt to me. Your story is a clear enough indication of your pain from the past. But still, I wonder who you are. I'm really troubled by your tendency to erupt like you do. I was so much in love with the "you" of the first days of our group, and so frightened by the "you" of the later sessions. I mean, because of the remarks like Bill being a ventriloquist to the recent comment on incest. Even someone as young as me sees the wisdom in letting sleeping dogs lie, but I want everyone here, including you, José, to know that these things about you are still very much here and now for me.

There is only a moment's pause before Tony speaks up.

> I am so much relating to you right now, Jewels. I am 'vibing' so much with you, as the cool young people say. And I am so proud of you because I see you living up to who you say you want to be in this group. I hope you keep on coming out like you have today. And José, I think you might have heard me wondering out loud before when I asked what was bugging you? I don't want to put you on the spot—I'm not looking for an answer in this moment, I just want you to know that the question is still in my mind.

Rick speaks up after Tony. He directs his comments to Chris, saying, "Chris, I'm still very curious about what caused you to leave us two weeks ago. I don't intend to throw you back into the past, but if any of the things that happened for you then are still with you now, I wonder if you could share them with me and with our group." Chris hesitates for a long moment and then says, "It's really interesting that you're bringing this up, Rick because I have a few things I want to say to you." Chris pauses, then takes a deep breath and continues.

> I perceive you as a quiet manipulator, sometimes even domineering, especially of women. Like, for example, you sending Ria to run after me instead of coming for me yourself, like you came for Bill. You have harshly rejected me from the very beginning of this group and when others have had positive feedback about my contributions to the group, you have not had a word of feedback to say.

By now Rick is hanging his head as he continues to listen. The mouths of other group members are agape with surprise as their jaws have nearly fallen to the floor. "I could not understand," Chris says in continuing, "Why you made such efforts to comfort José when Bill was hurting so much. And even when I came back last week, which I was very hesitant to do, you didn't welcome me back until the end of the session, and when you finally did it was in the most bland, unfeeling way." Chris exhales noisily and deeply after she finishes. Rick is shocked, but he tries to remain poised as he plays back to Chris some of what he has heard. In order to check whether or not he has understood her concerns accurately, Rick says, "You believe that I have harshly rejected you from the very beginning of this group." Chris nods. "You have noticed that when other group members had positive feedback about your contributions to the group, I have had none. And on these occasions I said not a word of feedback to you." Chris says, "Yes" and she continues to nod. "You took my actions in the case of the dispute between José and Bill as comforting José when it was Bill who was hurting. Apparently, you identified or related strongly to Bill in that episode." "Yes," Chris says, "I did." Then Rick says, "Another example of my rejection is shown in how I did not welcome you back two weeks ago until the very end of the session. When I finally did say something about your return, I did it in the most bland and unfeeling way." Chris continues to nod. "Then I demonstrated how manipulative, domineering, and I take you to mean 'chauvinistic,' I am by sending Ria out for you instead of coming myself, particularly since I had gone after Bill when he left the room." Chris says yes to everything. Rick says, "I truly regret that I have behaved in any such way as to cause you to doubt the sincerity of my actions. And even though you have given me some quite specific examples of my behavior, you haven't said much about your feelings. It seems to me that one thing you must be feeling is very hurt. Is that so?" Chris says, "Yes, very much so. I am deeply hurt." Then Rick says, "Is there any possibility I can redeem myself or is it an open-and-shut case against me?" Chris says, "You can redeem yourself, I guess. But I'm afraid you'll try to manipulate me as punishment for being honest." "It's interesting that you feel afraid," Rick says, "Because I do too. I feel afraid that you're not willing to hear what I intended by my actions. I'm also afraid that you're not willing to hear from me how I feel about you. Can we call upon group members to assist us in this? I am willing to trust their confirmation of any wrong thing I may have done that hurt you." Chris pauses, nervously clasping her hands together, but finally, she agrees. Rick says, "You have heard Chris's concerns, I would like to hear your observations and your experience of me with regard to Chris's points." Ria, who has hardly been able to contain herself, speaks up first and says, "If we start with presents things and work backwards, I'd have to say that when you came back to the group, Chris, we were already at the end of the session. Does anyone here take issue with Rick's words or attitude that night?" No member says anything. As Ria surveys faces, each member shakes his or her head. Rick says,

> Then in the matter of being chauvinistic in sending Ria out to you and comforting José when in your view it was Bill who needed comforting, let me say that I was more assertive in that meeting than I have been in some others, but I believed there was a safety risk because Bill seemed to be infuriated and he actually dove for José that night. Had it not been for Tony, the two men may have collided. I was with José only to keep him and others safe and in attempt to encourage him not to leave before we could find a temporary solution. Yes, I did ask Ria to go after you, but I did not intend it as an order. It was a chaotic moment. Group members were jeering at José. I knew that I could not leave the room and when I surveyed the room, Ria was looking into my face. Even though I asked her to go after you, it seemed she already knew what was needed. I never thought for a second that she needed an order from me.

In this way, Rick went through each complaint, seeking the perception of the group and their help in ascertaining which of the perceptions expressed by Chris were valid from the group's point of view, in light of whatever may have been occurring at one time or another when Chris reached the various conclusions she had. Doreen asked Chris if she had experience with other men who displayed Rick's characteristics. Chris answered that her father had several negative qualities in common with Rick. Her father was a highly controlling, domineering, and abusive man. Then Jewels inquires about the emotions that led Chris to leave the room two weeks earlier. Chris discloses that she had set José up as an ideal man. He was intelligent, funny, and independent, which she liked very much. She then noticed that whenever he failed to obtain his objective (something admittedly that was known only to him, Chris said), he responded by using cutting, sarcastic remarks to keep the upper hand. However, in José's episode with Bill, Chris's ideal view was shattered for several reasons. The first was that when José mentioned the word incest, it brought one of Chris's buried memories back to the surface wherein her elder sister, Katie, who is now deceased, told Chris when she came to live with her that she was molested by her father at age 16 and possibly impregnated. It was this incident that caused Katie to vow to be independent of both her parents and become self-supporting by age 18. Chris further discloses the ambivalent feelings of fear she had for her father. She also shared her sense of worthlessness in his eyes and powerlessness in her own eyes. She wonders if she will be helpless but to choose men who have her father's qualities. If she does this, she fears that she will then unconsciously recreate the worst for herself in relationships with men.

Chris explains that she identified with Bill's openness and vulnerability so strongly in the moment of his conflict with José that she ached. She also reveals that she had not told the group about being in recovery and that, too, created anxiety. She had been engaged in an incredible struggle to get free of her family and her alcoholic mother, who failed to protect her and her sister. She further says that when she came to the thought of disclosing her full story to the group and possibly getting a response like that given by José to Bill, it would be unbearable. "It was these kinds of horrifying thoughts that caused me to run from the room," Chris says as she breaks down and weeps, trying to speak through her weeping to say how embarrassed she is at her weakness. And also trying to say how foolish she feels for showing everyone what an absolute mess her mind and her life are. Then Doreen steps up and says,

> No one of us is perfect, Chris. You have been told by many people in this group that you have qualities that are very much appreciated by the group which are helpful to those you respond to and subsequently, helpful to our group. I hope that you can find the balance that is right for you, Chris. One in which you give yourself permission to embrace the good things you are and let go of some of the fearful predictions for yourself and overpowering self-blame. That's my hope for you.

Chris listens and nods but says no words in the moment. It seems that she tries to take in all that has happened and has been said. She glances at Rick. He smiles and says, "May I welcome you back to our group again tonight, Chris? You've done some powerful self-confrontation and taken some huge risks tonight. And you definitely had me on the hot seat. Whew!" Ria then says, "'Whew' says it all for me. I'd like to make a proposal before we use all of our time tonight. I propose that for the remainder of tonight's session we, the members of the group, call a moratorium on heaviness for the night." All group members responded with calls of "Here, here," around the circle. Then Chris speaks up and says,

> I don't want to stop the moratorium, but I have to say to you, Rick, that I'm sorry if I hurt you. I have so much missed seeing who you really are. The problem is that when I feel any hint of liking you or admiring you, which I do immensely, I automatically switch back into my emotional past. I was never in the now with you. I guess that's why I never saw the good person that you are. I've been locked up in my own horrific past. But because of you and this group, I'm aiming to be free.

Then Rick says,

> I'm very proud of you, Chris, and I'm so happy for you in your discovery. Now you have a chance to begin freeing yourself from some of the chains of your emotional past. You also have a chance to apply your discovery in other relationships outside our group. And when you do, if you notice that "beep-beeping" in your gut that signals a hint of your liking someone, you can stop and look to see who that person is before you allow all of the horrific stuff from the past to click in automatically and make you run away before you even see who it is that's there in front of you.

Then Rick continues,

> There are two more business items that I need to mention before we break. First, you all know that we have only three sessions remaining. This means that we are approaching termination. Everyone needs to think about termination before the end comes. If there are things you want to say, someone you want to connect with, or something you're unfinished with, think of who that person is you have unfinished business with and use the remaining time to finish it before the end comes. Think of everyone who is in our group and where you were the first night we gathered. How have your views and feelings toward members changed, grown more than you imagined, or not as much as you hoped? These are a few things to think about for termination. Also, there is one other bit of homework that I want you to do that I think will be enlightening for us as we move toward termination. As you reflect on the relationships you've formed with group members, I also want you to reflect on your families. I would like for you to construct families by placing members of the group into significant family roles. They do not have to represent current family members. They may parallel existing relationships or they may represent ideal relations. For example, you may choose someone to be the brother you wish you had rather than the one you actually have. Select a mother, father, spouse or significant other, younger or older sibling, grandparent, uncle or aunt, or cousin. If need be, you may even change people's gender. So begin to think about this and we'll pick up on some of your selections in our next meeting or two. Okay? Everybody travel safely. See you next time. Oh, by the way, remind me about the hot seat next time. I have a poem to share that's called "The Hot Seat."

Ending Stage Intersession Scenario Update: Session 13

In Session 13, themes of termination were highly prevalent throughout the night. Rick's having urged the group to "seize the moment" as the close of the group was drawing nigh appeared to have subterranean impact. Although, it was not clearly in members' conscious awareness, topic choices and the nature of interactions gave clear clues that there were concerns about the final transition. The mood of the session was exceptionally exuberant and members' spirits were very high. Members remembered the most positive aspects of past interactions, even where they may have seemed insignificant until now. In reflecting back on a time when he was considering fleeing from the group, Bill remembered something Tony had said in a low voice but loudly enough to be heard. "Yeah, I heard you behind me mumbling," Bill said. "But I didn't have a clue what you meant with that 'study long, you study wrong.' What the heck did you mean by that, Tony? Is that some philosophic words of wisdom for people with dilemmas?" Tony laughed. "Sounds to me like you got it, Bro. That's what my dad used to say when he had me stumped at the checker board. But I think you made a good move, Bill. For sure." Then Doreen teased Bill, calling him "sneaky eyes" for the looks he used to give to Ria. Doreen had members rolling in laughter as she made dramatic gestures, holding her arm across her face and peering over it with guilty-looking nuances saying, "Ladies and gentlemen of the jury, I ask you, 'Is this the face of a sneak?'" But Bill would not be outdone. He adapted a prissy posture and sucked his cheeks in so that his lips puckered.

He then gave his rendition of Doreen's first words to the group in his trademark breathy, mocking female voice while he glanced nervously at the floor, "Hi … I'm Doreen. I'm here because I'm an only child." Jewels then interjected, "You two may have missed your callings. You could both be theater majors." Then Jewels suddenly blurted an awkwardly timed question. "By the way, Doreen, I always wanted to ask you this but I always hesitated. Does it bother you that your brother is biracial?" Doreen paused as if she were stumped by the question. Finally, she said, "I can see why you'd ask. As I recall, it was the first thing I said in the group and I also said that he and I have the same father but his mother is Black. Wow. I never even heard that." Doreen looked at Ria and said, "Did you notice?" Ria bit her lip slowly nodded. "Sure, I did," she said. "But I didn't hold it against you. I always saw you as a good person who just didn't know." Doreen expressed how embarrassed she felt at not having noticed her words. She also confessed that her grandparents would never have supported an interracial marriage, much less an interracial affair. But she also said having had the experiences she has had during four years on a multiracial college campus; she believes that she could easily fall in love with and even marry someone of a different race or ethnic background than her own. She further said that she has made plans to contact her brother and embrace him as such because she had already learned that he is a really beautiful human being. Ria then said to Doreen, "See, I always knew you were good people, Ms. D. So ladies and gentlemen of the jury, I rest my case."

The group also made some forays into Rick's family role homework assignment. Some of the more surprising choices were José's assignment of Bill to the role of the brother he never had and Tony to the role of an uncle. Near the end of the group, Chris designated Rick as an ideal life partner, saying that she discovered her attraction to him by working through the assignment. She also said that she had considered placing him in a father role because of his authority in the group but she then realized that she could idealize him as a life partner because she now saw clearly that he was a good and decent human being and the kind of person she should aspire to have as a partner in life. The comment of the night came from the rather silent member, Youtu, who exclaimed just as the group was ending, "Will wonders ever cease!" The group members went out for coffee after the session at a local eatery where nachos and onion rings were reputed to be great. During the time the group members were in the restaurant, Tony and Ria got connected. When Jewels commented about how cozy they seemed, they disclosed to the group that in effect, they were becoming an item. Bill slumped down in the booth across the table from the pair, but he smiled and wished them all the best.

Ending Stage Scenario 14

During Session 14, group members go further with family roles enactment and also begin to tie up loose ends. Chris notices a connection between her sister Katie's death in a car accident and the death of Tony's father in a freak car accident. Bill mentions that he feels a strong connection to Tony's struggle after he was left in the care of a mean and hateful aunt. Bill says,

> Ria, I put you in my family as my spouse. But I know it's never going to happen. The day you gave that glowing feedback to Tony and he stared back at you totally speechless, I knew that your destinies were intertwined and written in the stars. But I had to do this for my own integrity, Ria, because I appreciate you so much. I see you as a good example of the kind of person I'd choose for a life partner and Tony, I think man, how lucky you are.

Ria blushes and says, "That's real sweet of you Bill and I thank you for letting me know. I think you are a good man and I hope you'll find your mate. Or maybe she'll find you." Ria giggles, and says, "I know that you already told us that 'you don't need nobody to tell you what to do and that you can take care of yourself' and so on, but I hope that you stay hopeful for good things to happen, Bill. Take it from me, you never know."

In spite of José's disclosure in Session 11, his interaction with Bill remains limited but not antagonistic. Rick receives a great deal of feedback during this session. The greatest bulk of it is positive. Almost every member named him to a paternal or uncle-like family position. One or two members select him as a spouse or life partner. Tony revealed that early on in the group he had gotten hints that members were puzzled about his apparent hostility toward Rick, who had been among the most compassionate in the room and who had actively worked in encouraging Tony not to "abandon the ship." Several members commented on how influential Tony's initially indecipherable remark about the planet sinking like a "freakin' *Titanic*" was. It had spawned many analogies to the water and the high seas. In speaking about his hostility, Tony says to Rick,

> I know you must've wondered why I was coming on so negative. I'm just going to give it to you in two words, Rick: My Dad. For Bill, dad was a monster in disguise, but for me, my father was the real deal, he was my hero. I have been kind of cautious ever since I lost him, but your beautiful, half-big-brotherly-half-young-father-like vibe was more than I was ready for at the time. But you're a beautiful brother, Rick, so I have to give you some love for that. It's funny because when I was hostile, I was dealing with whether to let you in or not. Now that I have accepted our connection, I've got to deal with letting you go, and that's the hard one for me.

There is a quiet moment or two after Tony's feedback to Rick as the group hums along in a kind of bittersweetness. Jewels then speaks up and says, "Since we are talking about water and high seas analogies, I just can't help but remembering the session when Bill was leaving the room and Ria, you yelled out 'Man overboard!' When I saw you do that, girl I definitely knew you were special."

The group works hard to keep some semblance of work going in the group, but the reminiscent themes make it apparent to everyone that group members are in denial. Everyone feels the impending conclusion washing over the group like a stormy wave splashes onto the shore. Ria notices José moving like he might begin to speak, so she speaks up before him. "I really have to tell you all this," she says.

> I have been having a recurring dream about a woman standing at a doorstep saying goodbye. I cannot tell if it is my mother or me. But I know that

something about leaving this group is very hard. I'm already missing being here. I'm so sad the end is near. The dream makes me see that I have been dealing with a secret fear of being alone my entire life. But at least by now I know I'm worth being loved. And the fear is not as big as it used to be.

Seconds after Ria, José erupts and says, "I can't hold it in. … I can't stand it any longer. I need something from this group." All eyes turn to José but no one says a word. Chris and Jewels both unconsciously cross their arms. Rick looks around and no one is moving. Finally, you speak up and say, "Okay, José. I'll ask the question. What is it that you need?" José sits on the edge of his chair and says with undeniable sincerity, "I need redemption from you all. Since I made the mistakes I made, my life has been a wreck. I can't leave the group like this."

Rick says, "I never believed in throwing the baby out with the bath. I believe that if you can see into this issue of how your pain and denial contaminate your present potential for relief, renewal, and connection, you might leave this group with a powerful awareness to take into your social relationships outside this group. As for your redemption, each one has to choose. But I'm happy to say that I forgave you two weeks ago and I forgive you now." Then Bill says, "Me, too." Then Jewels crosses the room to plant a kiss on José's temple and says, "I forgive you." Then Ria says, "Forgiven." Then Doreen, Chris, Tony, and you each in turn forgive. José doesn't weep but his eyes are filled with tears of relief and realization. It is apparent to everyone that change has happened in José's consciousness and change has happened in the room.

Finally, Rick tells members that there will be a pot-luck celebration at the end of next week's meeting. He also mentions that he will ask members to complete a form anonymously that is included in members' information packets for evaluation of the group and its leader's effectiveness. Doreen will collect them and deliver them to the counseling center director's office on Rick's behalf. Rick goes on to say, "Next we'll do any remaining family placements and we'll make a head-on acknowledgment of the closing of our group. So that's it for now. See you all next time."

Then in the final seconds, Doreen says, "Rick, what about the poem? You never told us last week. Can you tell us now before we go?" Rick smiled and said, "I thought I was going to escape, but I guess not. So here's the poem as I wrote it the first time I was in a counseling group."

> I am on the Hot Seat
> For all of you to see.
> I feel my heart's beating,
> And I feel me.
> My ache is insisting,
> I'm running away.
> I keep on resisting,
> The price I must pay.
> I've got to go through it,
> Though dying of fright.

I know I must do it,
In hopes that I might
Become the real me.

Ending Stage: Scenario 15

In this meeting, members gather for Session 15, the final session of the group. Members enter the room with a lot of chatter and the mood is light. A table off to the side fills up with assorted homemade dishes, as well as name-brand pizza, soda, and other kinds of snacks including fruit and vegetables for healthy eaters. There are a few family assignments that members have not yet gotten to. This includes you and José. You are quite surprised at the roles you are placed into by your peers and after you see how they have placed you into their idealized families, you take the placement assignment more seriously as you place members into your family. You are especially touched by Jewels, who tells you that she really wishes that she had reached out to you more because she sees you as a valuable member she failed to connect with as much as she could have. You also receive some feedback from Doreen, Tony, and Ria, who teases you about some of your interactions with "Slumping" Bill and his misdirected anger in the early weeks of the group.

Ending Stage: Scenario 15 Alternate Ending A As the meeting continues, it seems as if a heavy cloud comes over the group. Members attempt to make light chitchat without any noticeable effort to turn inwards toward any kind of reflection. There is a lot of surface chatter about how members will keep in touch after the group disbands. Everyone knows there are layers of stuff and feelings unaddressed, but no one makes any initiative to explore them. E-mail addresses are exchanged with assurances that they will inseparably link together those who trade them. There is also a lot of laughter, sometimes laughter that is too loud and empty sounding. In some ways, group members seem to be regressing back several weeks into the past. They rebel against completing evaluation forms for the group as if they are resurrected counterdependent rebels. They refuse to do anything because they don't "cow-tow" to anyone or anything representing authority. Even though these members ooooh and aaahhh over every dish that is placed on the table, they hardly eat anything. They glance at their watches two or three times a minute, and when the ending time finally is near, they cannot wait to get out of the meeting room.

Ending Stage: Scenario 15 Alternate Ending B As the meeting continues, it seems as if a heavy cloud comes over the group. Ria says, "Has anybody noticed how heavy the room feels?" Tony breaks into a line from a Temptations' song, "Oh how I wish that it would rain, sunshine blue sky, please go away." Doreen pipes up, "Uh-uh, Tony we don't need to wish for rain to hide any teardrops. I know the song. It was written before I was born, but my freshman-year roommate was an oldies but goodies nut." Several people chuckled.

"I'm feeling the heaviness too, Ria." Doreen says. "I've shared some real fears about being alone. It's ironic because I never reached out in the past. You guys helped me face my fears. I see that I can reach out to escape the grip of my fears by letting others know my feelings, hopes, and reactions. I'm going to miss this group—a lot."

Doreen is soon joined by Jewels and Chris, who has entered the room with a small duffle bag. Bill spies the bag and cannot resist teasing. "Hey Chris, whatcha got in that bag? Did you bring us some real special snacks or what?" Chris retorts, "Can anyone believe this man? With all of the food on the table there, Bill is wondering if some other food is in my bag. Bill, I'm going to recommend that we extend the group a week because you are too unique and valuable to let go of. Don't worry about my bag. I have a surprise in there for everyone."

Then José speaks up to say,

> I feel very grateful for your patience with me. The things I have learned from all of you will help me live a better life. I am leaving this group acknowledging every connection that I have felt with anyone here. And I am taking away something I did not understand until I came here of how much self-created loneliness I have suffered. I see it now, and I finally feel like I'm ready to stop doing this to myself and blaming others for my misery.

Several members nod their heads. Ria is the only one who gives a verbal response as she says, "Good for you, José. I hope your realization takes you far along life's road."

Then Rick says, "I'm sad that our group is ending. I feel really bonded with this group and I will miss being here with you. I am so proud of your accomplishments and insights. You have all grown so much through struggle. I will miss you all." Rick suggests that it is time to close the group and says that now is the time when each person must face the fact that this group, which has spent an hour and a half each week for the past three months, will not be meeting in the future. Then Jewels says, "I agree with Tony, Rick. I feel so grateful for what I've learned from you. Your impact is huge in my book. I know I'm going to have a huge hole in my life when I won't see you once a week anymore."

Rick further suggests that each member make one statement of something they appreciate or something they regret. Members do this with no hesitation. Things said to be appreciated include Rick's presence, Bill's humor, growth through struggle, self-discovery, friendship, listening, acceptance, mutual support, laughter and tears, discovery and unearthing of hidden personal powers, and such things as these. Things regretted include failure to use time as fully as one might have used it, not having taken bigger risks sooner, fleeing from fears, being controlled by anger, not loving oneself enough, not reaching out to others more, not having been in a group before now, not understanding how big here and now is, and such things as these. At last, Rick asks the final question: "Is there anything else hanging at this time?" Now Jewels erupts, "Ria, I almost forgot. I wanted to tell you that I read that book you mentioned, *Finding Fish*. All I can say is that I think I understand you better and Miss Pickett was something else!" Ria and a few other members smile and then Rick says, "I declare that this group is now closed. I hope that each of you will take the best of what you've experienced and learned here into your lives and relationships beyond this group. Happy transitions, everybody!" Group members write thoughtful evaluations and hand them over to Doreen. And as members drift to the food table to take up paper plates to serve themselves and have their last lighthearted chats, Doreen unpacks a keyboard from her duffle bag. She sets it up on a small table and begins to play a personally inspired tune. No one knew what a sweet and powerful voice she was gifted with until she sings the words:

> Now its time to go, but I'm happy that we're all friends
> When we met at first I was so fearful about letting you in
> But now my heart is spread open as wide as the skies
> How wonderful when love touches you and opens your eyes
> It's just incredible how huge one little moment can be
> One feels that little drop contains an ocean of eternity
> I'm so grateful now for the time we were able to spend
> With all my heart, I hope that our friendship never will end

Multicultural Considerations: Ending Stage

When Session 12 begins there is a slight bit of tension in the atmosphere and members begin with the usual ice-breaking chitchat. Jewels is the first to initiate, and what she says has surprising multicultural implications. After making some brief comments about seeing her contributions to the group as limited and now not wanting to be limited anymore, she shares how she has felt herself more involved as she has reacted to things happening in the group. Jewels then reveals to Ria that she sees her as the person in the group to whom she feels the strongest connection. But Jewels also shares what she has been embarrassed to tell Ria because she feared she would be seen by Ria as "the little White girl" who has no clue about suffering and struggling in the world to survive. Jewels tell Ria how greatly moved she is by her story. Understanding that Ria's mother had given her away, Jewels attempts to tell Ria how much she believes she deserves to be kept and her hopes to be Ria's friend. Ria's response is powerful and heartfelt. She apologizes to Jewels for interjecting her reaction and says that she does not see Jewels as a color, that she notices her color, yes, but does not judge her by it. Then Ria shares that even though she is Black, the best foster mother she ever had is White. Ria also says to Jewels: "You *are* my friend." It is interesting that Jewels continues to give feedback to other members around the group. It appears that such significant disclosures between Jewels and Ria are worthy of more attention in the moment. It may be that Jewels' self-created agenda, important as it is, might be poorly timed. However, Jewels' questions are part of the same challenges of awareness that any effective group member must face, namely: When to initiate? When should I wait? When and how should I listen? How should I respond?

Jewels continues around the group with poignant feedback to José and a disclosure of how "in love" with him she felt but how frightened and disheartened she became. Tony relates to Jewels and speaks up to let her know. He encourages her to keep on coming out with what she thinks and feels.

Rick says to Chris that he doesn't want to push Chris into thoughts of the past but also he says that if any of the things that happened before in the group are still with her, he wonders if she would like to share them with him and the group.

After a long hesitation, Chris tells Rick that she has a few things she wants to say to him. She takes a deep breath then launches into a disclosure of feelings and perceptions of Rick that leave him stunned. Chris tells him that she perceives him as a manipulator and as someone who dominates women. She tells him that he has rejected her since the beginning of the group and she accuses him of withholding feedback from her and, most especially, positive feedback. Chris then tells Rick that when others have had positive reactions to her contributions, nothing had been forthcoming from him.

Group members are completely stunned by Chris's assault on Rick, who is by now completely crestfallen and silenced. He attempts to remain poised while telling Chris what he has heard. She acknowledges that he has heard her correctly, at which time Rick expresses regret to have behaved in such a way as to cause Chris to doubt his sincerity. He also acknowledges the hurt she must feel, which she affirms as quite deep. Rick asks Chris whether there is any possibility that he might redeem himself and though she says yes, she expresses fear that Rick will attempt to punish her for being honest. Rick expresses his own fear that Chris will simply remain unwilling to accept any explanation of what he intended by his actions. He asks Chris if he can call upon the group for help and also says that he will accept their confirmation of any wrongs he may have done. Chris is nervous but accepts.

Ria is the first group member to respond, and she leads the group through a review of several interactions, working backwards from present to recent to past events. No other member took issue with Rick's behavior. When asked about Rick, each member shook his or her head, saying they had no issue with him. Utilizing the support and assistance of the group for reviewing each of Chris's complaints, Rick sought feedback and member perceptions of his initiatives in the group. Doreen's explorations with Chris as to her past experiences with other men who had Rick's characteristics led to a watershed of insights for Chris, not the least of which were those connected to her sense of powerlessness in relationship to her father. Upon reaching this point, Chris was completely exposed and vulnerable. Still, she finds nothing except empathy, support, acceptance, and understanding from fellow group members. Doreen was brilliant in reminding Chris that no one is perfect and encourages her to seek balance in embracing more of the good things she is and letting go of some of the fearful negative expectations and self-blame.

The interactions between Chris and Rick, the leader, and among Rick, Chris, and the group at large, have much value when considered from the point of view of Bowman's (1996) multicultural training. One can see that the power of self-awareness, intrapersonal insight, and learning adds clarity in the midst of cross-racial and cross-gender interactions that might simply never reach resolution if seen only from the point of view of ethnicity, race, or gender. In each case, exploration from the perspective of race plus self-awareness, gender plus self-awareness, ethnicity plus self-awareness leads to insight that is expansive, obstacle-shifting, and possibilities-opening. Such a perspective fosters possibilities for intrapersonal revisioning and discovery and new levels of interpersonal learning and growth. The wisdom of intrapersonal struggle, awareness, and insight that is so much a possibility to be gained is so much a guide to how more satisfactory group relations can be advanced in the classroom, in therapeutic situations, and perhaps in the world. One sees the value of struggle with oneself instead of struggling only with the other members.

Themes of termination are highly prevalent in the intersession scenario update for Session 13. It is clear that group members are aware that termination is near. The mood is exuberant and spirits are high. Members remember and review significant group interactions of the past with much lighthearted teasing and playfulness. Members also venture into activities related to the family members role assignment exercise. Several members see connections between their own experiences and those of others. Bill asks Tony about his comment: "Study long, you study wrong" and learns about Tony's dad. Doreen teases Bill about his "sneaky eyes" and does a playful impression of him looking around the group. Bill, however, bounces back with an impression of Doreen that is hilarious. He does an impersonation of Doreen's breathy voice with his lips puckered in the way he sees her. Later, Jewels asks Doreen if she is bothered by the fact that her brother is biracial. Doreen sees her early remarks in the group about having a brother whose mother is Black in an entirely new light. She tells the group that she now has plans to contact her brother and attempt to establish a relationship with him because she has heard that he is a really good and beautiful person. She also reveals that based on her diversity experiences during her college years she believes that she could easily fall in love with and marry someone of a different race or ethnic background.

It is significant that near the end of the group, Chris places Rick in the role of an ideal life partner and idealized father. She shares with Rick and the group that she has come to clearly seeing Rick as a good and decent human being. She says that she also sees that he is a person with the kind of qualities she aspires to have in a life companion or spouse. Tony and Ria also acknowledge a mutual romantic interest in each other during this session.

In Session 14, group members go further in sharing how they had placed various members into roles in their families. As group members go further in this process, a great many connections are made. Members see similarities between various life experiences, their own and those of others. In this way, members gain deeper insights into crises they had navigated in the past. During this session, Bill shares how he sees Ria as an ideal life partner and confesses his regret that she was not destined to be with him instead of Tony. Rick receives a great deal of feedback during this session and is named to a meaningful role as a father or uncle figure in many instances. In at least two cases, he is named as an ideal spouse or life partner. One of the most powerful disclosures in the session comes from Tony, who shares that his past negative-seeming reactions toward Rick were because he saw both brotherly and paternal connections with Rick to his own deceased father, whom he loved. Tony also reveals that the thought of opening his heart so wide to any man made him fearful of loss again. Tony's feedback to Rick clearly has powerful emotional impact on everyone present in the group.

Ria continues to be a powerful presence in this session as she continues to make heartfelt and insightful disclosures. Members forgive José, and his eyes fill with tears of understanding and relief. In Session 15, the last session, Youtu and José, who have not shared about their family placements, have their final chance to do it. In Alternate Ending A for Session 15, members stay on the surface of interpersonal contact and engage in empty chitchat. They avoid any discussion of feelings and cannot wait to leave the room. In Alternate Ending B, Ria notices the mood of the group and Doreen initiates a disclosure about fears of being alone. Other members, including Jewels, Chris, and José, speak up to share how much value the group has had for them. Rick helps group members to acknowledge more directly that the group is ending and puts members into a closing activity that enables them to transition into closing by expressing what they appreciate and regret about the experience having now reached this point.

From the perspective of Bowman's (1996) model for multicultural training, the interactions of group members throughout the sessions of the ending stage are filled with richness because members have learned the value of self-knowledge. Connections that members make to the experiences of others demonstrate the power and beauty of the idea that as knowledge of oneself increases, likewise, acceptance of others also increases. Examples of this are especially evident in interaction between Chris and Tony, where Chris notices the connection between her sister's death and the death of Tony's father, both in car accidents. Another example is seen in Doreen and Bill's connection through playfulness and impersonations. The identifications by almost all members with Rick as a father or uncle are yet another example. It is exceptionally apparent that during the course of the group members are continuously making discoveries and learning about themselves and other members. Finally, however, it is very interesting to notice that in terms of how one relates to others, one gains insight into the aspects of how the ethnicity-related and cultural experiences of others shape their psyche and view of the world. In the direct interpersonal contact of the group, with diverse others, members experience the meaning of what Bowman (1996) describes as moving from being one who knows that cultural differences exist to being one who knows how to interact effectively and with self-confidence to others who are culturally different from oneself. What appears to happen is that in the process of learning through meaningful interpersonal contact, members evolve a way of relating that is transracial, transethnic, and transcultural. The racial, ethnic, and cultural realities are no less important, but the human being moves more clearly into the foreground and one's humanity becomes most prevalent. In group circumstances where intrapersonal intentions for the good are held by each member, there is hope that the cream of what it is to be human will rise to the top.

QUESTIONS FOR SCENARIO REVIEW

1. What are your reactions to the scenario?
2. Are you surprised by Chris's perceptions and reactions to Rick? What is your understanding of the process or processes occurring between Chris and Rick?
3. What has been the most meaningful part of the scenarios for you?
4. What self-discoveries have happened for you?

5. Which members do you relate to most easily? What qualities or characteristics cause you to feel as you do about them?
6. Which member would be the most difficult for you to relate to or respond to with empathy?
7. What is the significance of forgiveness? Were you ready to forgive José?
8. Why did group members not talk of termination and related ending concerns during Alternate Ending A for the final session?
9. Where was the leadership for the group's ending session? What are your reactions to Rick?

PART 1 PROLOGUE TIPS FOR THE ENDING (TERMINATION) STAGE

Key Components of an Effective Member Mindset

Keep in Mind the Interactive Processes of Group Work

- An effective member notices which issues and related themes are most prevalent in the group interaction.
- It is important that you actively attempt to observe what happens between yourself and other group members.
- It is helpful to notice what happens between yourself and the group leader, what happens between yourself and the group, and what happens to you within the context of the group as a unit or system.

Learn How to Think in Process Terms and Distinguish Between Content and Process

- As an effective member, you are encouraged to develop an ability to notice what is happening in the one or other of the dimensions (content or process) or what is happening simultaneously in both.
- In effective groups where content and process are in balance, group members experience the content as inherently more dynamic and living regardless of the nature of themes or topics.
- Process is the activating cause of meaningful and facilitative interaction in groups.
- When groups are experienced as flat, slow-moving, and lacking energy, the explanation usually has to do with process.

Open Yourself to Discovery

- Openness improves possibilities for increased self-awareness and discovery because it clears channels for receiving information.
- Constructive openness involves risk and benefit. You are continuously choosing and taking changes one moment at a time.
- What you face may be exhilarating or horrifying.

- Understanding more about the impact of your presence and personality, power, weaknesses and strengths, about your lovability, and talent is the kind of discovery that groups have to offer.
- Exploration through initiatives of risk or sharing, examination, or disclosure holds the possibility for increased self-knowledge, discovery, insight, and liberation from the grip of unresolved past personal history.
- Gaining insight by seeing aspects of our personality and ways of relating that were completely unknown to us really means discovery (Luft, 1969).
- Deep discovery and realization can lead not only to change but to transformative growth.
- Constructive change and positive ideas about your abilities, potential, and worth can open completely new and unexpected avenues in your life.

Understand the Purpose of the Group

- Through the process of interaction, you will have opportunities to gain counseling, interpersonal communications, and self-awareness skills through the activities of the group.
- You will have many opportunities to discover things about yourself in terms of what your strengths are in your relations with others and what the impacts of your particular style of communication are.
- You are also likely to discover things about your personal power as well as your fears.
- You will have a chance to acquire strategies for dealing with challenges and crises in your life, for being more productive in situations of conflict, and for fostering growth and positive change in others.
- It may be helpful to begin think of what you would like to achieve or accomplish in the group that may be helpful to you in your life.
- Consider outlining some goals for yourself that you might begin to look at in the group.

Check Your Attitude
- It makes things better all around if you want to be in the group and have a good attitude about the possibilities of getting something positive for yourself.
- Asking yourself whether you are interested in being in the group is a good first question (even at a later stage of the group).
- Have you been mandated or required to attend for some personal or health-related reason? If you did not choose to come, you may still decide how you want to use your time in the group.
- If you are coming into the group with the feeling of being forced, it may still be helpful to acknowledge your unwillingness, lack of interest, or resistance and attempt to reframe them.

- The ability to shift and flex can be a tremendous personal asset. It might be helpful to try using your unwillingness to your own advantage and to the group's advantage as well. Even if you happen to be an unwilling participant, your case is not a lost cause.
- It may be helpful to understand that your personal feelings and reactions can be keys to your effectiveness.
- I invite you to make a conscious decision to notice your feelings and reactions and use them constructively in the group.
- If you are entering the group because you are genuinely interested in discovering more about yourself, if you are interested in how to deal with the unique challenges of your life and circumstances, and also interested to know more about how others see you, that will make it all the better.
- The challenge or work to be done is to remain aware of yourself in the present moment and time. Remaining aware of yourself includes noticing your thoughts, noticing your feelings and bodily reactions, and possibly even noticing your silence or lack of reaction to what other members (including the leader) say and do.

Cultivate Conditions Within That Foster Growth for Yourself and Others

- An effective participant is always seeking balance between his or her own inner-focused development and relationships with others in the group.
- A participant who grasps the significance of this process develops attitudes and ways of being within that have observable impact in their activity, initiatives, and contact with others in the group.
- A facilitative, growth-engendering attitude reflects three qualities. Namely, these are congruence, empathy, and unconditional positive regard (Rogers, 1961).

Choose to Become a Group-Work Apprentice

- An apprentice is a person who is interested in achieving mastery in his or her field of pursuit.
- Mastery refers to a level of development where skill, knowledge, and experience flow together with who you are as a person.
- This "flowing together" is commonly referred to as *integration* or the *integral* or *integrative* dimension.
- Any apprentice who seeks mastery must qualify for entering apprenticeship by three steps, which are: (a) interest; (b) openness to discovery; and (c) willingness to change.
- If you have these qualities, you may begin. After you begin you must negotiate the lessons, challenges, and difficulties faced by apprentices of the past.
- You must bring the outcomes and insights of the learning process into your current awareness and presently lived experience.

- As a qualified apprentice, your experience in the group draws you through a journey that provides possibilities for dynamic insight and growth.
- The extent to which you achieve insight, growth, and integration corresponds directly to your dedication to the three steps of interest, openness to discovery, and willingness to change.

PART 2 PROLOGUE TIPS FOR THE ENDING (TERMINATION) STAGE

Basic Strategies and Skills for Successful Involvement in the Group

- Be here now
- Listen and reflect
- Learn to convey and receive feedback
- Initiate consistently to avoid fading into silence
- Express feelings as feelings
- Utilize the three-lenses approach for practicing skills and staying involved
- Monitor your personal process
- Track your awareness, discovery, and learning by keeping a journal

5

Leaders and Group Leadership

PURPOSE OF THE CHAPTER

*T*he purpose of this chapter is to increase your awareness of the qualities possessed by effective group leaders and also to inform you of what is required of you as a group member who may have an interest in becoming an effective group leader. However, this chapter is not predicated on making every reader a leader. Even though qualities such as self-confidence, self-awareness, awareness of others, and capacity to initiate consciously in critical moments are important for leaders, these qualities can be equally powerful for people who only seek to be members, who are interested in working collaboratively with others who share their interests. Additionally, this chapter presents the concept of sought membership (Shakoor & Rabinowitz, 1978), a model that describes how individuals in person-group relationships as members can achieve leadership through the membership process. An experiential section, which utilizes scenario excerpts to be reviewed from the perspective of leadership functions, follows the sought membership discussion.

THEORETICAL SECTION

What Is Leadership?

Leadership in the context of counseling, therapeutic, and other experiential groups refers to the skillful utilization of self-awareness, knowledge of interpersonal relationships, group process and group norms, as well as an understanding of conflict and communication, in order to facilitate the following capacities in members: self-awareness, interpersonal communication skills, and the ability to relate with honesty, balance, and effectiveness with other persons within group situations. It is important you remember that leadership requires initiative as it relates to prescribed responsibilities and leader functions. Effective leadership ultimately rests upon your ability as a person to balance how to be with what to do.

About the Person Called the Leader

From the member's point of view, the group leader or facilitator is often seen as one of the most powerful, provocative, enigmatic, challenging, and confusing persons in the group. Early on, it may be helpful for you to notice how you are thinking about the designated leader in your group and how you are relating to him or to her. What are your first impressions? When you found yourself sitting in the group for the first time, what did you expect to happen? How did you think leadership would be demonstrated? What did you think you needed personally in order to make a good start in the group? What were you expecting in terms of direction, guidance, and support? What ideas did you have about what the leader should do?

By now, I suspect that you are aware that in most groups, participants come with the expectation that someone takes charge. New members are likely to feel uncomfortable and, on some occasions, even annoyed if there is no clear direction, no specific agenda, or topic to be discussed. In certain kinds of groups, such as counseling groups, therapy groups, psycho-educational groups, and a variety of experiential or personal-growth types, a clear purpose usually exists. However, varying degrees of ambiguity, direction, and lack of structure are designed into the process. Even though you may find it difficult, it is important for you to understand that the leader's objective is not to frustrate you or make you uncomfortable on purpose. In most groups that are organized for personal growth of some kind, the leader's aim is usually focused on a few things. These include interacting with you and your group in ways that foster and facilitate your self-awareness and self-confidence. Also included is your ability as a leader to stay balanced and focused in moments when things are not clear and direction from others is not forthcoming. Even though it may feel frightening, frustrating, or anxiety-provoking to adjust and grapple with such a process, there are some benefits you can take away. Learning to be here and now, noticing your thoughts, feelings, and reactions while you are in the process, can help you to accomplish the following things:

1. You can experience the group and its individual members, including yourself, as a unit; gain insight into the process; learn to trust it; and evolve toward increased self-awareness, improved interpersonal competence, and transformational growth over time.
2. You can experience an increased sense of personal empowerment and freedom by discovering how your ways of relating to authority facilitate or block your potential.
3. You can experience your own capacity to become an effective leader through your experiences as an effective group participant.
4. You can increase your understanding of the challenges and rewards of group leadership and how you can become a leader if you are interested in pursuing it.

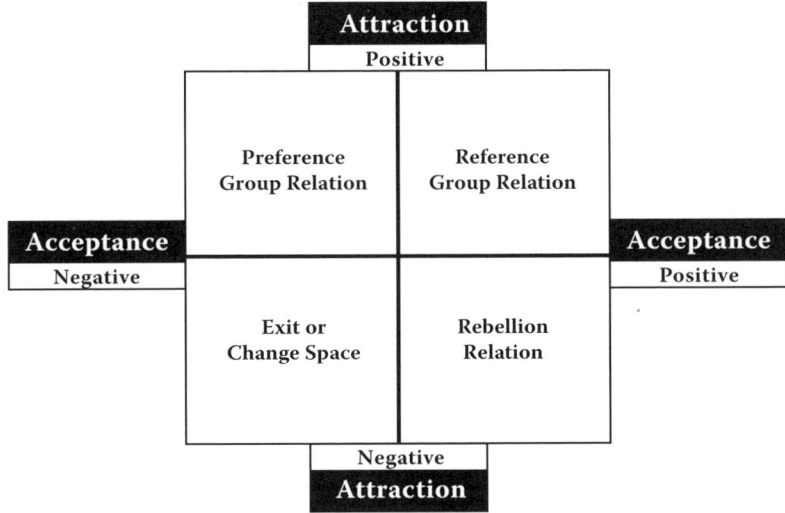

Figure 5.1 Sought membership model.

The Concept of Sought Membership

I would like to present here Shakoor and Rabinowitz's (1978) sought membership model, which describes the relationship between individuals and groups and the dynamic process of membership (see Figure 5.1). The model applies only to those groups in which the individual actively seeks membership and provides a view of how members can achieve leadership. Counseling, therapy, experiential, and other groups may qualify for this model, provided that members of such groups seek to belong. Other groups include fraternities, social clubs, societies, and other special interest groups.

Description of the Sought Membership Model

Because membership is dynamic and person-group relationships are in a state of constant motion, any membership model must be able to reflect the movement simultaneously and quickly and capture a view of the relationship between the person and the group in any moment in time. The sought membership model attempts to complement and build upon the work of Jackson (1959), who presented a general conceptual framework for describing various types of psychological membership in groups based on the concepts of attraction and acceptance. The sought membership model is different from Jackson's in that it simplifies the description of the person-group relationship and additionally specifies leadership functions and the role of norms and includes elements of change and time that suggest temporary occupation of one category and category shifts.

In Jackson's (1959) model, internalization of group norms becomes the prerequisite for psychological membership. Norms determine the parameters for prescribed individual activity within the group. Entry into the space of psychological membership means that the member who arrives there becomes a model of the norm for members outside of that space who are seeking entry into it. For example, in the scenarios for group stages, Rick is clearly the legitimate designated leader, but Maria, the group member who likes to be called Ria, is an aspiring leader and the scenarios detail many of her initiatives that support group norms and model effective member behavior. One of her memorable initiatives is that she shouted "Man overboard!" when Bill was at risk of leaving the group and Rick, the leader, sprinted after him. Ria's initiative demonstrates a spontaneous example of meaning attribution, caring, and executive aspects of leadership functions. José's expression of his outright envy of Ria because she seemed to always know "the right thing" to do in the group is an example of the caring aspect of leadership. I will discuss these aspects further and provide other examples later.

After becoming a model of the group norm for psychological membership, the individual who has achieved it becomes a force in the "power field," which is Kurt Lewin's (1944) language for the energy that maintains group equilibrium around norms relating to psychological membership. It is at this point in the sought membership model that the psychological member assumes a leader role. Such a member, therefore, becomes the role prescription for others actively seeking membership, acceptance, leadership, and influence in the group. In the sought membership view, the concept of leader role is compatible with definitions of leadership presented by Carter (1953), who proposed five distinct views, including (a) the leader as the focus of group behavior; (b) leadership in terms of group goals; (c) the leader as the person so named by group members; (d) the leader as the one who most influences group members; and (e) the leader as one who engages in leadership behavior. Kline (2003), also presented a description of essential attitudes and objectives that "can reduce the complexity of the group leadership task" (p. 173), summarized in the following ideas:

1. Direct members to interact with each other. This means that the leadership role focuses on the facilitation and orchestration of interaction.
2. Establish and reinforce the personal responsibilities of members for learning and interacting congruently.
3. Help members develop interpersonal boundaries that allow the communication of feelings and the disclosure of perceptions.
4. Challenge the group to develop here-and-now norms and sufficiently closed external group boundaries.
5. Strike a balance between technical expertise and presence as a person. Leaders cannot develop an effective learning environment without establishing their presence as an open, authentic, and direct person.
6. Engage members in identifying avoided interactive concerns and work diligently to involve the group in confronting and resolving them.
7. Continuously demonstrate the attitude *that members and not leaders* are the primary source of therapeutic change [*emphasis mine*].
8. Act with confidence in the belief that members are capable of dealing effectively with difficult, emotionally charged interpersonal issues.

The Sought Membership Concept of Attraction

Positive attraction in the sought membership model is defined, therefore, as a person's attempt or willingness to assume some of the functions of leadership within the group. Negative attraction is defined as a person's shying away from leadership functions or attempts to subvert other members from assuming them. The degree to which the individual exerts energy to the performance of these functions will determine how positively he or she is attracted to the group. Examples of leader behavior functions correspond to those of Lieberman, Yalom, and Miles (1973). These are summarized as primarily four basic functions: emotional stimulation, caring, meaning attribution, and executive function. Emotional stimulation "represents leader behavior which emphasizes revealing feelings, challenging, confrontation, revelation of personal values, beliefs, frequent participation as a member in the group, exhortation, and drawing attention to self" (Lieberman et al., p. 235). Caring functions "involve protecting, offering friendship, love, affection, and frequent invitation for members to seek feedback as well as support, praise, and encouragement" (Lieberman, Yalom, & Miles, 1973, p. 238). From a stylistic perspective, caring leaders express considerable warmth, acceptance, genuineness, and a real concern for other human beings in the group. Meaning attribution is a way of making sense of behavior by "cognitizing" it, as is said in Lieberman et al. That is to say, providing concepts for how to understand, explain, clarify, and interpret behavior and also providing frameworks for how behavior can be changed. Executive function focuses on the administrative aspects of group leader tasks. These are defined "in terms of behaviors such as limit-setting, suggesting or setting rules, limits, norms setting goals or directions of movement, managing time, sequencing, pacing, stopping, blocking, interceding, as well as such behaviors as inviting, eliciting, questioning, suggesting procedures for the group or person and dealing with decision-making" (Lieberman, Yalom, & Miles, 1973, p. 239).

The Sought Membership Concept of Acceptance

Positive acceptance in the sought membership model is defined as the group allowing the individual to assume leadership functions. A positive relationship means that the group permits or looks to the individual to perform these functions. In a negative acceptance relationship, the group does not allow an individual to perform these leadership functions and might even work to subvert the activity.

Reference Group Relation

The upper right-hand space of Figure 5.1 refers to an individual-group relationship in which the individual is positively attracted to the group and positively accepted by the group. This means that the individual has attempted with a great deal of energy to assume a number of leadership functions. Because this relationship is one of high acceptance, the group allows the assumption and performance of leader functions.

Within this space the individual has completely internalized the group norms and has become a model of such norms for other members, outside of this space, who are actively seeking entry into it. The individual is now able to exert an influence on the group that has, to a degree, made him or her act within the parameters of actions acceptable to the group. It is at this point that the individual becomes a force to maintain the parameters by rewarding other members for proper action and reprimanding others for improper action.

Preference Group Relation

The upper left-hand space of Figure 5.1 refers to an individual-group relationship in which the individual is positively attracted to the group but negatively accepted by the group. This means that the individual is attempting to assume some of the leadership functions but is not being allowed to do so by the group. In this space the individual has begun to model the example set by the reference group member in an attempt to become more positively accepted by the group.

Rebellion Relation

The lower right-hand space of Figure 5.1 refers to an individual-group relationship in which the individual is negatively attracted to the group but positively accepted by the group. This means that the individual is looked to by the group to perform some leadership functions, but the individual is unwilling to do so. In this space, the individual would attempt to subvert the activities of the group and attempts by other group members to assume the functions of leadership.

Exit or Change Space

The lower left-hand space of Figure 5.1 represents a choice point (Glidewell, 1970) for both the individual and the group. It describes a situation in which the individual is negatively attracted to the group and negatively accepted by the group. Within this space an individual must decide whether to remain a member of the group and to accept the group norms or leave the group. The group must decide whether it is willing to modify itself to accept the individual or whether it is willing to let the individual leave.

You should also understand that in addition to defining group member attempts to assume leadership and the group's allowing a member to assume it, the concepts of attraction and acceptance also describe any group member's state of psychological membership, according to which quadrant of the sought membership matrix he or she falls. Therefore, when you are in the reference group relationship to the group, you are in the highest state of psychological membership.

EXPERIENTIAL SECTION

This section presents scenario excerpts that highlight various group member initiatives over the course of the group. As you review them, consider where you

LEADERS AND GROUP LEADERSHIP   89

might place the particular group member within the sought membership matrix and what aspect of the leadership function is exemplified by the person's initiative. You may review the following excerpts alone, with another group member, or in a small group.

Chapter 1: Beginning Stage Examples

1. In this excerpt from Scenario 1, assess Rick as leader when he welcomes group members: One or two of the strangers say "Hi" and Rick greets you warmly. He addresses you by name and says, "I'm glad you could come." Rick introduces himself to the group and talks about his graduate studies and his interest in the counseling field. He also explains the purpose of the group as one of sharing about one's experiences, whether broad or limited, on a multicultural campus in a multicultural world. Further, he says that other objectives are to learn about the experiences of others and to forge new connections.
2. In this excerpt from the beginning of Scenario 2, Rick welcomes members back for Session 2. After everyone is settled he says, "Hello everybody, It's good to see you back. How are you all doing today?" Assess Rick as leader when he responded to Doreen, who had made a last-minute disclosure toward the end of the first session. Rick noticed her disclosure and her affect, but he also realized he had further obligations to establish norms for beginning and ending on time: "It appears to me," he said, "that your discovery about your father's relationship with another woman who bore him a son, whom you're just learning about twelve years or more after the fact, is something that is having quite an impact on you right now." "Yea-aaah," she said. "I wish I had the words to say how much it has affected me. My world has definitely been rocked and I feel like I've been blessed and cursed at the same time." "I'm very thankful for what you've shared with us," Rick said. "I hope that we can make this group a place where you and others can share your feelings and concerns. But right now, we're at the end of our time for this session. I want to thank you all for being here. I look forward to seeing everybody next time."
3. In this excerpt from Scenario 2, assess Bill's initiative. Tony has made his unforgettable comment: "Why do people have to go through so much pain? This world is nothing but a freakin' *Titanic*." Bill makes an early appropriate initiative and beats you (Youtu) to the punch when he sits up and says to Tony: "I can relate what you say about people going through pain. It's obvious that the world is like you said, 'a freakin' mess.'"
4. Assess Rick in this excerpt from Scenario 2. When Tony realizes that everyone is looking at him and shortly thereafter stands up and says, "I gotta go. I mean, it was nice to meet you but I'm all messed up. I've got to leave." Rick immediately speaks up and says,

   You're absolutely free to go if you have to Tony but I wish you'd stick around. It sounds like there are things happening now or that have happened before that are really on your mind in here. You'd being doing us all a big favor if you stuck around. Man, I see your hands shaking and what you said was kind of cryptic, but it sure hit me with power and it probably hit others in here too. I wonder if you'd be willing to put off leaving and hang in here with us for at least another session. It would be great if you would share a bit of what happened here that led you to say the things you did. I wonder if you'd be willing to hear more from Bill and others who seem to be affected by what you said.

5. Assess Rick's initiative in this excerpt from Alternative Ending A to Scenario 3: When José introduces himself, he tells that his surname is Banderas and Chris asks if he is related to the film star, Antonio Banderas. Rick looks on all the while, but the members seem to ignore him. The group atmosphere becomes light, almost like a bottle of champagne was just popped. The group descends into a round of heady chatter about upcoming movies and half the members are participating. The only ones on the fringes of this discussion are Doreen, Bill, Tony, you, and Rick. Finally, Rick speaks up and says, "I'm very happy to see folks trying to get things going in our group, but I wonder if group members notice what's gone on in the last ten or fifteen minutes. Perhaps it feels very nice, but really it's missing the target in terms of what actually needs to happen here." Group members appear to be stunned by Rick's comments.
6. Overall reflection question: Having assessed and placed the initiators in the excerpts above, if you were asked to switch roles with any of them in their particular situations, which would you choose and what would you do similarly or differently?

Chapter 2: Early Middle Stage Examples

1. In this excerpt from Chapter 2, Scenario 4, assess Chris's initiative: Doreen has reminded everyone how Bill had spent almost the entire first two sessions slumped down in his chair. Chris speaks up on Bill's behalf to remind opponents that he (Bill) had expressed sympathy for Tony early on, even if his comments were not expressed in the "proper form."
2. Assess the initiative of José in this scenario. Following Chris's comments above, José then says, "I don't see that there's anything so great about Bill's reaction to Tony. Bill is like a ventriloquist who speaks through other people. The problem is, though, that you never really know what his message is." The scowl that took over Bill's face suggested that he is infuriated by José's words. "Man, you just need to shut up," Bill said. "You don't even know what you're talking about. Where do you get off calling me a ventriloquist? I don't know where you're coming from with that." The tension in the group is apparent and José does not back down. "From what I see," José says,

the first time Tony spoke, you rode in on his feelings, saying that you could relate to his pain and you agreed that the world is a freaking mess. Then you rode in again on Youtu's words when he or she asked what the heck was happening? You responded with words like, "I don't need nobody to tell me what the heck to do 'cause I can take care of myself just fine." Personally, I think Youtu was right. Even though your words really appeared to be meant for Rick, you gave your anger to Youtu.

3. Assess the following initiatives of Tony and Chris as Bill is about to storm out of the group room: Bill stands up from his chair and says, "I'm outta here." When he turns to leave the room, Tony speaks up and says, "Think about it, man." Bill's expression turned to exasperation as he says, "I hear you man, but I'm just not fitting in here." Chris then passes an unopened bottle of water to Bill and says, "We all get thirsty in the desert or when our ship is lost at sea." Bill does appear to be lost as he stands there. Tony picks up on Chris's language and says to Bill, "How about sitting down, Bro?"
4. In this excerpt from Scenario 4, assess Rick's initiative: Outside, Rick is attempting to get Bill to delay his decision. "Maybe you will decide that you don't want to be in this group," Rick says. "But if I had to judge by the expressions on the faces of everyone in that room, I'd say that even though every one of them doesn't like your attitude and how you say the things you have to say, not one of them wants you out of the group. I think it would be great to learn more about what makes you feel satisfied or not about how you are fitting into the group."
5. In this excerpt from Chapter 2, Scenario 6, assess Youtu: After José, Doreen, and Chris spontaneously share that they have gained a lot of insight too because they each knew that they had a lot of family baggage, you then tell Chris that you appreciate her sharing because you had hopes of getting to know more about her. You also tell her that you find her sense of timing in the group really effective in creating movement. You give the example of her comment when passing a bottle of water to Bill in his moment of distress.
6. Overall reflection question: Having assessed and placed the initiators in the excerpts above, if you were asked to switch roles with any of them in their particular situations, which would you choose and what would you do similarly or differently?

Chapter 3: Late Middle Stage Examples

1. In these excerpts from Chapter 3, Scenario 8, assess Ria and José. Ria and Tony decide not to discuss their first impressions of each other in the café but bring the discussion back to the group instead: In the group, Ria speaks up and says,

When Tony and I were in the café, we told each other some of the first impressions we had of each other in the group. We decided to do that because it wouldn't involve talking about any of you behind your backs. So Tony suggested that we tell you guys our first impressions and maybe we can get more feedback. If other folks want to talk about first impressions, maybe we can do that too.

José speaks up and says,

Talking about first impressions really sounds interesting but in some ways—and I know I'm sounding a bit like Rick, but I think it's just a little off target. How about if people really want to talk about impressions, we make it now impressions and so long as people don't go overboard with "then and there" stuff, they can add in some first impressions.

2. Assess Chris's initiative in this excerpt for Scenario 8: Chris speaks up during a pause and says, "I'm interested in two things right now. I'd really like to hear more from Jewels and Ria about how you relate to Becky and Celeste in Doreen's family. The second thing is I'd like to receive feedback from the group about how you see me now." José speaks up instantly. "Chris, I see you as one of the most supportive members of the group. If there's anybody here who can stretch their dollar, so to speak, I'd say it's you."
3. In this excerpt from Chapter 3, Scenario 9, assess Rick and José. José has been continuously sarcastic. Tony tells him that he has been different and wonders if José's changes of mood are connected with something inside or outside the group: José answers, "It's really a bit of both. I'm going to just cut to the chase for everybody though. Believe it or not, I have my own 'issues' but I'm not comfortable about putting them out in this group. Also, I thought this was supposed to be a personal growth group, not psychoanalysis." Rick looks up and calmly says,

You are free to choose like everyone else here, José. No one is going to try to force you. So thanks for saying as much as you've said. On another front, it seems like the group is having a hard time getting started tonight. A lot of good things happened before. I believe good things can still happen now. So let me just say this and I'll leave each of you to decide where we go from here. If anyone wonders what is happening in the group, the answer is always going to be the same for how to find out what that is. Every group member has to say to her- or himself the following sentence: The way to get at what is happening in the group is to get to what is happening with me.

4. Assess Rick's initiative in this excerpt for Scenario 9. José's sarcastic question to Bill regarding incest is infuriating. Rick has to intervene to prevent a physical confrontation: While the group is challenging José and attempting to calm Bill down, Chris flees the room weeping. Rick notices and asks Ria to go after her. Ria pursues her all the way outside to the parking lot, but Chris reaches her car and speeds away as Ria stands helpless in the fumes. When Ria returns to the group, the group has reconvened and Bill and José are standing behind their chairs on opposite sides of the room. Rick has taken a very strong position in the group about safety and asks everyone to stay for 15 minutes longer to attempt some kind of resolution.

He insists that José cannot leave the room until making an apology that Bill can hear and possibly accept. José looks remorseful and Bill is beginning to calm down.

5. This excerpt is from Chapter 3, Scenario 11. José is confronted in the group session after he has a highly conflictive encounter with Bill. He would like to flee, but Ria physically blocks his path. Rick intervenes with both José and Ria. Assess Rick's initiative: Rick says,

> I'm going to ask you not only to step aside, Ria. I'm going to ask you to open the door wide. And José, I'm going to ask you to choose like we have not seen you do before. I am asking you to let us know that part of you that said those words to Bill and let us really be with you and hear you. Or you can choose to stuff your painful things inside and walk through the door pretending we never existed.

> Rick looks at Ria and says, "Ria, I respectfully implore you to step away from the door. And José, I ask you to choose."

6. Overall reflection question: Having assessed and placed the initiators in the excerpts above, if you were asked to switch roles with any of them in their particular situations, which would you choose and what would you do similarly or differently?

Chapter 4: Ending (Termination) Stage Examples

1. In Scenario 12, Jewels gives feedback to José regarding his past behavior in the group, particularly his episode with Bill. Assess Jewels' initiative in the excerpt:

> I also want to say to you, José, that I'm stunned by your behavior in the group. Your apology to Bill sounded heartfelt to me. Your story is a clear enough indication of your pain from the past. But still, I wonder who you are. I'm really troubled by your tendency to erupt like you do. I was so much in love with the "you" of the first days of our group, and so frightened by the "you" of the later sessions. I mean, because of the remarks like Bill being a ventriloquist to the recent comment on incest. Even someone as young as me sees the wisdom in letting sleeping dogs lie but I want everyone here, including you, José, to know that these things about you are still very much here and now for me.

2. Assess Doreen. Later in Scenario 12 she speaks up when Chris breaks down and expresses her hope for Chris: Doreen steps up and says,

> No one of us is perfect, Chris. And you have been told by many people in this group that you have qualities that are very much appreciated by the group that are helpful to those you respond to and, subsequently, helpful to our group. I hope that you can find the balance that is right for you, Chris. One in which you give yourself permission to embrace the good things you are and let go of some of the fearful predictions for yourself and overpowering self-blame. That's my hope for you.

3. Assess Rick in this excerpt from Scenario 12. After a highly intense interaction with Chris in the previous session, she glances at Rick to check his reaction to her: Rick smiles and says, "May I welcome you back to our group again tonight, Chris? You've done some powerful self-confrontation and taken some huge risks tonight. And you definitely had me on the hot seat. Whew!" Later in the same meeting Rick says to Chris:

> I'm very proud of you, Chris, and I'm so happy for you in your discovery. Now you have a chance to begin freeing yourself from some of the chains of your emotional past. You also have a chance to apply your discovery in other relationships outside our group. And when you do, if you notice that "beep-beeping" in your gut that signals a hint of your liking someone, you can stop and look to see who that person is before you allow all of the horrific stuff from the past to click in automatically and make you run away before you even see who it is that's there in front of you.

4. Assess Rick again in the excerpt from Scenario 12. After his comments to Chris, he reminds the group members that time is running out: Rick says,

> There are two more business items that I need to mention before we break. First, you all know that we have only three sessions remaining. This means that we are approaching termination. Everyone needs to think about termination before the end comes. If there are things you want to say, someone you want to connect with, or something you're unfinished with, think of who that person is you have unfinished business with and use the remaining time to finish it before the end comes. Think of everyone who is in our group and where you were the first night we gathered. How have your views and feelings toward members changed, grown more than you imagined, or not as much as you hoped? These are a few things to think about for termination.

5. Assess Youtu in this excerpt from Scenario 14. José has expressed that he needs something from the group, but no one wants to ask the question. You (Youtu) step up to do it: José erupts and says, "I can't hold it in. ... I can't stand it any longer. I need something from this group." All eyes turn to José, but no one says a word. Chris and Jewels both unconsciously cross their arms. Rick looks around and no one is moving. Finally, you speak up and say, "Okay, José. I'll ask the question. What is it that you need?" José sits on the edge of his chair and says with undeniable sincerity, "I need redemption from you all. Since I made the mistakes I made, my life has been a wreck. I can't leave the group like this."

6. Overall reflection question: Having assessed and placed the initiators in the excerpts above, if you were asked to switch roles with any of them in their particular situations, which would you choose and what would you do similarly or differently?

6

A Word on Ethical Concerns

*E*thics have to do with principles of right or good conduct. In group work, ethical principles deal with accepted rules or standards governing professional behavior. In the case of counseling, psychology, social work, and other helping professions, these principles most often apply to the behavior of members of a profession toward those who are being served. From your perspective as a group member it is important that you have an awareness of ethical behavior, in the interest of not doing harm as well as in the interest of self-protection. Usually in group situations, the greatest burden falls upon the designated leader. If the group takes place in an academic context, it usually falls to the course instructor. Therefore, I encourage you to do your utmost to remain aware of your personal intentions and to know and understand the purposes of the group that you are joining. You must have the understanding that you can participate in whichever group you enter with safety and with confidence that you can maintain personal integrity with regard to your personal values. You must also understand that you will carry a responsibility to demonstrate respect for the worth and values of others.

NOTICE YOUR MOTIVATIONS AND INTENTIONS WHEN YOU ENTER THE GROUP

Do not become a victim of "group think." Sort out your reasons for entering the group you are entering. If you have no previous group experience (beyond being in your own family), ask someone's advice. However, if you are mandated, do not prejudge the leader based on your view of the entire system within which she or he functions. However, do remain self-aware and open your eyes and your mind as you attempt to see how you can benefit and possibly make a contribution.

EXPLORE CREDENTIALS BUT ALSO TRUST YOUR GUT

Explore the credibility of organizations presenting groups, especially in the context of consumer therapy or personal growth. Explore the leader's credentials and reputation and do not hesitate to explore the grapevine. Regardless of what others say, pay particular attention to your personal gut instincts and trust yourself.

BE AWARE OF YOUR PERSONAL VALUES

Your values are fundamental to who you are as a person. It is essential that you know what your beliefs are, what you consider important for yourself, and what you believe about others. It is normal in counseling and therapy groups to expect that your values may be challenged. This means that you may be encouraged to examine or assess what your values are or how your values impact your life and relationships with others. However, it is not correct for you to advise other group members on what to do regarding their values or beliefs, nor should they give you advice.

BE RESPECTFUL OF YOUR OWN PROCESS AND THE PROCESS OF OTHERS

Understand your personal psychological makeup and basic learning style. Even if your group is operating within time-limited parameters, recognize that growth and learning, healing and discovery, gaining insight, and overcoming blockages are all processes that unfold over time. There are moments of thunderous epiphanies and other long stretches that feel like no progress will ever happen. Learn to recognize what process is. Respect your own process. Do not undermine your own process or that of others. Especially do not do it for the reason that what you hope for is not available in the moment, either from yourself or for yourself or possibly from or for the other person. Also know the difference between being helpful and being an enabler.

INTERSECTING ISSUES

Such things as forced touching and inappropriate catharsis are at the intersection of process and values. Your personal values regarding space and contact may be examined, but they should be respected in the group, as you should respect these things related to the values and preferences of others. Sometimes cultural mores are involved.

Inappropriate catharsis, which means "leader or member-forced" emotional releases, may be both inappropriate and unethical. Counseling, therapy, and other experiential group settings typically have highly charged emotional periods but never emotions simply for the sake of emotionality. No one should be told "you must cry or scream" in order to pass or for something healing to happen unless it is a primal therapy session. In this regard, knowing your own gut is critically important with regard to how you share in the group. In spite of the fact that initiative is hugely important and fundamental, do not force yourself into unnecessary overexposure.

KEEP TO INTEGRITY AND CONFIDENTIALITY

Stand up for yourself and what you know is right for yourself, but do not impose your values. Understand that each member has his or her own goals for the group. Be very careful with regard to the negative potential of subgrouping. It can subvert and sabotage the process of the group. Expect not to be exploited and never exploit the vulnerability of others. Often in counseling, therapy, and other personal-growth groups, you may be more privy to intimate aspects of other people's lives than you might be in most other situations. Honor the trust that you have been given in your role as a member in the way you would like to be honored.

If you would like to know more, follow the link for Assocation for Specialists in Group Work standards regarding the training of group workers (2000) and especially see the link for the American Counseling Association's code of ethics (2005).

Bon Voyage! I wish you good luck.

Appendix A

GROUP MEMBER GUIDE SHEET (FOR INTERPERSONAL FEEDBACK AND SELF-CORRECTION)

Use this form for personal assessment and planning; also use this form for assessment and feedback to others. Rate yourself or rate another member on a scale of 1 to 5. (1–2 = *little or poorly*, 3–4 = *fairly well or good*, and 5 = *very well [often] or excellent*)

Rating	Skill
_____	Understands components of an effective member mindset
_____	Understands basic strategies and skills for successful involvement in the group
_____	Makes consistent demonstrable attempts to apply an understanding of components, strategies, and skills in interaction with others
_____	Conveys feedback constructively and consistently
_____	Solicits feedback periodically
_____	Receives feedback without being defensive
_____	Pushes past anxiety when in conflict and remains engaged
_____	Utilizes feedback to become more productive in interpersonal interactions
_____	Takes ownership of (and distinguishes between) thoughts, feelings, and beliefs
_____	Is a good role model for what an effective group member should be
_____	Demonstrates willingness to address authority issues and points of personal struggle with the process
_____	Has gained new awareness of defenses and commits to taking higher level risks
_____	Is consistently facilitative in her or his initiatives
_____	Displays leadership potential

Components, strategies, and skills I'd like to work on or suggested that I/you work on.

1. _____
   _____
2. _____
   _____

Appendix B

ADDITIONAL MULTICULTURAL RESOURCES WORTH REVIEWING

Film

- *Nā Kamalei: The Men of Hula* (2007) Lehua Films
- PBS Previews: "The Quilts of Gee's Bend" (February 2005)
- *When the Road Bends: Tales of a Gypsy Caravan* (2006)
- *The Native Americans* (1994) documentary; highly recommended
- *My Architect: A Son's Journey* (2003) Nathaniel Kahn
- *Frida* (2002) Julie Taymor
- *Rivers & Tides* (2001) Andy Goldsworthy
- *Maya Lin: A Strong Clear Vision* (1995)
- *Jane Goodall's Return to Gombe* (2005) incorporates music and musical instruments such as cello, Ibo drum, flute, guitar, ilahis (Sufi chants) and different kinds of music from various cultures
- *The Journey of Man* (PBS), an amazing film that echoes and further synthesizes so many of my thoughts, feelings, intuitions, understandings, wisdoms, and reflections. To trace the migrations of humanity is fabulous. To look into the eyes of the San Bushman and see features and hints of all the races within his face is one moment that makes this film quite special.
- *Antwone Fisher* (2003) Full screen edition

Books

- *The Native Americans: An Illustrated History*
- *Beaches*, Gideon Bosker and Lena Lentek
- *The Book of Elders: The Life Stories & Wisdom of Great American Indians*, as told to Sandy Johnson & photographed by Dan Budnik
- *Wings of Delight*, poetry edited by Robert Bly
- Rumi's poetry as translated by Coleman Barks; "Say I Am You" and others
- *A Little Book on the Human Shadow*, Robert Bly
- *The Four Agreements*, Don Miguel Ruiz
- *Prisons We Choose to Live Inside*, Doris Lessing
- *Mutant Message*, Marlo Morgan
- The Carlos Castenada series
- *The Iceman*, Don Lessem and documentaries related to the Iceman
- *Sufi Cuisine*, Nevin Halici
- *Foods of the Southwest Indian Nations*, Lois Ellen Frank
- *FlatBreads & Flavors*, Jeffrey Alford and Naomi Duguid
- *The Autobiography of Malcolm X*
- *Down These Mean Streets*, by Piri Thomas

- *Native Son,* by Richard Wright (any of his works)
- *Harlem: What Happens to a Dream Deferred? Does It Dry Up Like a Raisin in the Sun?* by Langston Hughes

Appendix C

FOCAL CONFLICT THEORY

Focal conflict theory (Whitaker, 1989) is useful for both group members and prospective group leaders. Understanding focal conflict can be especially empowering for you as a group member by providing you with a model for making sense of the complexities of group interaction in a simple and comprehensible way. Focal conflict theory will show you the value of noticing your own thoughts, feelings, and reactions to other group members and demonstrates the surprising interrelatedness of members in their shared concerns, on both conscious and subconscious levels. In addition to providing you with ideas about conflict and anxiety in groups and interpersonal interactions, the theory shows how these can be understood, resolved, and utilized to the benefit of the group and each of its members.

Focal conflict theory was presented by Whitaker and Lieberman (1964), whose ideas for the theory sprang from the work of renowned social scientist Kurt Lewin. It is also advantageous that this theory has been highly empirically researched, so if you want to explore its further application, you can explore this through sources, many of which give examples directly from group sessions.

Whitaker and Lieberman (1964) suggest that conflict exists in counseling, therapy, and other types of groups because undisclosed aims, secret wishes, private hopes, and personal concerns that members want to address in the group compete with their unexpressed fears about what will happen if they allow their concerns and wishes to become known. In the first instance, the motives that represent the undisclosed secret wishes are coined *disturbing*. In the second instance, the motives that represent the unexpressed fears are coined *reactive*. Thus disturbing motives are in conflict with the reactive motives. Together, the pair of motives reflects the shared concerns of the group. Therefore, your ability to notice your own unexpressed concerns and to notice which themes are most dominant in group sessions will give you insight into one or even a series of possible group focal conflicts and hints of the related disturbing and reactive motives that create them. For example, a group member Loretta is haunted by painful memories of an adolescent eating disorder (her disturbing motive), which she conquered for several years but recently relapsed back into when she began to have marital difficulties. She wants to obtain help from the group and desperately wants to share her feelings, but in order to do so she must confront her fears that the group will hate and reject her (her reactive motive) if she discloses that she is not only going through a painful divorce but she is secretly dealing with her pain by binging and purging.

GROUP SOLUTIONS

Because groups, in similar ways as its individual members, are limited in their ability to tolerate sustained anxiety and tension, the group naturally attempts to

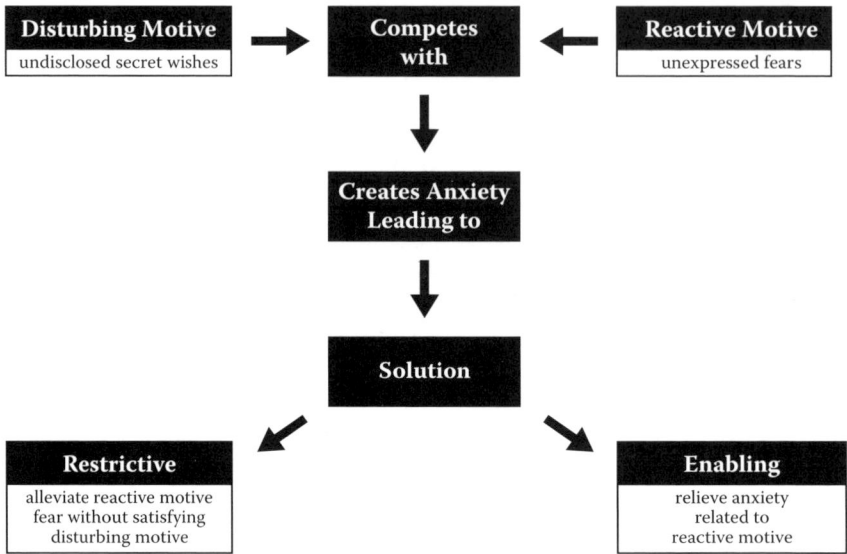

Figure C.1 Focal conflict theory.

discover an acceptable solution to existing focal conflict. Whitaker and Lieberman (1964) identify two types of solutions, *restrictive* and *enabling*. In order for a group solution to be successful, it must first be accepted by full-group consensus. Secondly, it must reduce the anxiety, particularly with regard to the group members' abilities to address the disturbing motive.

Enabling solutions are so named because they help to relieve the anxiety that is related to the reactive motive, which in the example of Loretta is her fear that the group will hate and reject her. Restrictive solutions are those that alleviate the fear associated with the reactive motive but do so without any satisfaction of the disturbing motive. This is accomplished most often by simply avoiding the discussion about disturbing and reactive motives. These include the undisclosed aims, secret wishes, private hopes, and personal concerns that members hope to address in the group or their unexpressed fears about what will happen if they let their fears become known (see Figure C.1).

In discussing group solutions, Whitaker and Lieberman (1964) give an example of another aspect of group solutions, which they describe as *solutional* conflict. Such conflict occurs when members cannot agree on a solution to a particular focal conflict. Subsequently, members' competing views lead to the solutional conflict. In the example, during the first group session of an inpatient group, several patients expressed interest in revealing their faults to the group (the disturbing motive); however, there was also expressed some fear of the kind of criticism, particularly from other patients, that might follow such self-exposure as this (the reactive motive). The group was beginning to hit upon a provisional solution wherein a majority of the group was coalescing around the idea that because not one of them was perfect, they should all agree to tolerate one another's shortcomings. This solution was immediately blocked by one patient's insistence that he indeed *was* perfect. Much energy in the group was then directed toward getting the "deviant" patient to change his mind, but he refused to budge. A solution eventually emerged when one group member commented that each of them was a "perfectionist" in the sense of trying to improve him- or herself and this went unchallenged by the deviant patient. However as sophistic (or hair-splitting) and semantically tortured this resolution might appear to be, it seemed to genuinely work as a group solution in that at this point in the discussion tension began to clearly abate; the patients had reached a tentative consensus to the effect that though they constituted a quite superior group in some ways, they could still each hope to gain some personal benefit from the group experience. This solution therefore left some room for a further exploration of what some of their individual difficulties might be.

Appendix D

HELMS'S CONCEPT OF RACIAL IDENTITY

Because of the significance of these concepts as they relate to multicultural development and awareness, I am providing a summary of Helms's (1993) discussion of racial identity followed by Helms and Cook's (1999) Table 1: A Summary of Common Ego Status Themes; Table 2: White Racial Identity Ego Statuses, Examples, and Information-Processing Strategies (IPS); and Table 3: Summary of ALANA (People of Color) Racial Identity Ego Statuses, Examples, and Information-Processing Strategies (IPS) in the following appendices. *ALANA* refers to People of Color, including African Americans, Asians, Latinos, and Native Americans.

SUMMARY OF HELMS'S DISCUSSION ON RACIAL IDENTITY

In Helms's (1993) view, *racial identity* is a term referring to an individual's "sense of group or collective identity based on one's perception that he or she shares a common racial heritage with a particular racial group" (p. 3).

She further says that "racial identity development theory concerns the psychological implications of racial group membership; [namely,] that is belief systems that evolve in reaction to perceived differential racial group membership" (p. 4).

She explains that "Black and White (now People of Color and White) identity theories examine psychological development from the level of racial rather than ethnic similarity" (p. 785). She mentions Casas (1984), who points out that ethnicity is not biologically defined; therefore, race and ethnicity are not the same. Helms (1993) further says that

> racial identity also refers to the *quality* or manner of one's identification with respective racial groups. Racial identity theories, therefore generally describe a variety of modes of identification. Black racial identity theories attempt to explain the various ways in which Blacks can identify (or not identify) with other Blacks and/or adopt or abandon identities resulting from racial victimization; White racial identity theories attempt to explain the various ways in which Whites can identify (or not identify) with other Whites and/or evolve or avoid evolving a non-oppressive White identity. (p. 5, italics added)

Helms (1993) explains that "one's quality of adjustment has been hypothesized to result from a combination of 'personal identity,' 'reference group orientation,' and 'ascribed identity'" (p. 5).

- *Personal identity* concerns one's feelings and attitudes about oneself; in other words, generic personality characteristics such as anxiety, self-esteem, and so on.

- *Reference group orientation* refers to the extent to which one uses particular racial groups; for example, Blacks or Whites in this country, to guide one's feelings, thoughts, and behaviors. One's reference group orientation is reflected in such things as value systems, organizational memberships, ideologies, and so on.
- *Ascribed identity* pertains to the individual's deliberate affiliation or commitment to a particular racial group.

Helms (1993) explains that one can choose to commit to one of four categories if one is a person of color (POC) or White: POC primarily, White primarily, neither, or both. Hence, a person who considers one race or the other to be the important definer of self has a *monoracial* ascribed identity; a person who feels connectedness to both racial groups has a *biracial* identity; and a person who commits to neither group has a *marginal* ascribed identity. Helms says that it also seems possible that each of these components varies relatively independently. So, for example, a POC or White person might feel positively about himself or herself, treat the experiences of racial group members as irrelevant to his or her own life circumstances, and feel a commitment to neither racial group.

> [The] assimilating Black (i.e., the Black person who wants to become a non-distinguishable member of White society) for instance, might feel good about herself or himself (i.e., positive personal identity), while attempting to live according to "White" beliefs about the world (i.e., the person who believes everyone should be defined by the tenets of White socialization experiences), use Whites as a reference group for defining appropriate behavior (i.e., White reference-group orientation), and feel commitment only to other Whites. (i.e., White ascribed identity.) (Helms, p. 6)

Helms (1993) further explains that

> the three components—personal identity, reference group orientation, and ascribed identity—undoubtedly interact with each other. For instance, to the extent that society stereotypes one racial group as "dirty," or "shiftless," and "ignorant" and another as "clean," "industrious," and "intelligent" and can enforce such stereotypes, then it is likely that the individual will find it easier to use the second rather than the first group as both a reference group and source of ascribed identity. Relatedly, if one identifies with the positively characterized group, then it is likely that one will feel more positively about oneself than if one does not. However, such identifications become problematic to the extent that they require denial or distortions of oneself and/or the racial group(s) from which one descends. (p. 6)

Appendix E

TABLE E.1 Summary of Common Ego Status Themes in Helms's Racial Identity Models[a]

Themes
Persons must overcome societal definitions of one's socioracial group by redefining oneself in personally meaningful terms
Self redefinition involves a sequential differentiation or maturation of ego statuses[b]
Simplest or least complex statuses develop first
The seeds of more complex statuses are inherent in earlier statuses
Statuses that are most consistently reinforced in the environment become the strongest and potentially dominant
A status is dominant when it occupies the largest percentage of the ego and is used most frequently for interpreting racial material
Statuses that are not reinforced recede in importance and become recessive
Recessive statuses are infrequently used to govern responses to racial stimuli
Ego statuses are hypothetical constructs that cannot be measured
The strength of ego statuses is inferred from their behavioral expressions—schemata
Schemata typically reflect the themes that are present in the person's socioracial environment(s)
Environments can be internal (psychological) or external (environmental)

[a] From *Using Race and Culture in Counseling and Psychotherapy* (1st ed.), by J. E. Helms and D. Cook, 1999, p. 85. Boston: Allyn & Bacon/Merrill Education. Copyright 1999 by Pearson Education. Reprinted with permission.

[b] A *status* is similar to a developmental level or stage. Each level is characterized by cognitive, affective, and connotative "intrapsychic" principles that guide an individual's response to racial stimuli in his or her internal or external environment.

Appendix F

TABLE F.1 Summary of White Racial Identity Ego Statuses, Examples, and Information-Processing Strategies (IPS)[a]

Status	Example
Contact: Satisfaction with racial status quo, obliviousness to racism and one's participation in it. If racial factors influence life decisions, they do so in a simplistic fashion. IPS: Obliviousness, denial, superficiality, and avoidance.	Example: "… The Balls have prided themselves on the ancestral image of compassion, emphasizing that masters tried as best they could not to separate slave families in sale; that no Ball masters perpetrated violence or engaged in master-slave sex. Ed Ball's research is viewed by some family members, especially the elderly ones, as a threat to long-held beliefs. Some would prefer not to know too many details about their ancestors' slave practices, one relative says" (Duke, 1994, p. 12).
Disintegration: Disorientation and anxiety provoked by unresolvable racial moral dilemmas that force one to choose between own-group loyalty and humanism. May be stymied by life situations that arouse racial dilemmas. IPS: Suppression, ambivalence, and controlling.	Example: "I was upset. I couldn't do anything for a couple of weeks. … Was I causing more pain than healing? Was this somebody else's history, not mine? Was I an expropriator, as Stefani Zinerman [a Black woman newspaper editor] accuses me of being? Should I stop [investigating my family's history of slave ownership] and let black [sic] people do their own history?" (Duke, 1994, p. 12).
Reintegration: Idealization of one's socioracial group; denigration and intolerance for other groups. Racial factors may strongly influence life decisions. IPS: Selective perception and negative outgroup distortion.	Example: "When someone asks him, 'Don't you feel bad because your ancestors owned slaves?' his response is 'No, I don't feel bad because my ancestors owned slaves. I mean, get over it. If Ed wants to go around and apologize, Ed's free to go around and apologize. But quite frankly, Ed didn't own any slaves. He isn't responsible for slavery or anybody's misfortunes …'" (Duke, 1994, p. 24).
Pseudo-Independence: Intellectualized commitment to one's own socioracial group and subtle superiority and tolerance of other socioracial groups as long as they can be helped to conform to White standards of merit. IPS: Selective perception, cognitive restructuring, and conditional regard.	Example: "He has also said to them [the descendants of his family's slaves]: I am sorry … his mother, brother and a few other relatives believe the apology had a healing effect …" (Duke, 1994, p. 12).
Immersion: The searching for an understanding of the personal meaning of Whiteness and racism and the ways by which one benefits from them as well as redefinition of Whiteness. IPS: Hypervigilence, judgmental, and cognitive-affective restructuring.	Example: "I'm interested to look at whiteness as carefully as white people look at blackness. As a white person, I'm interested to understand how my ethnicity has produced me as an individual … and how whiteness produces the majority experience of Americans. My plantation research might be a way for me to do this intellectually as a writer" (Duke, 1994, p. 12).

Continued

TABLE F.1 Summary of White Racial Identity Ego Statuses, Examples, and Information-Processing Strategies (IPS)[a] (*Continued*)

Status	Example
Emersion: A sense of discovery, security, sanity, and group solidarity and pride that accompanies being with other White people who are embarked on the mission of rediscovering Whiteness. IPS: Sociable, pride, seeking positive group attributes.	Example: "But Ed's apology [for his family's ownership of slaves] produced positive reactions as well. Janet and Ted Ball, Ed's mother and brother, both were moved by [his apology]: 'I was crying too,' says Janet Ball. ... Ted Ball ... says he whispered a private 'thank you' to his little brother. ... He feels grateful to Ed 'for doing the hard work it took to get to the apology'" (Duke, 1994, p. 24).
Autonomy: Informed positive socioracial group commitment, use of internal standards for self-definition, capacity to relinquish the privileges of racism. Person tries to avoid life options that require participation in racial oppression. IPS: Flexible and complex.	Example: "... It's [the exploration of his familial history of slave ownership] about me personally trying to find some way as a white person, quite apart from my family's history, to acknowledge what's happened in this country. I mean during the time that English-speaking people have been in this country, for more years were black people enslaved than not enslaved" (Duke, 1994, p. 25).

Note: Descriptions of racial identity statuses are adapted from Helms, J.E. (1994) Racial identify and other "racial" constructs. In E.J. Tricket, R. Watts, and D. Birman (Eds.)., *Human Diversity* (pp. 285–311). San Francisco: Jossey Bass. Racial identity ego statuses are listed in the order that they are hypothesized to evolve.

[a] From *Using Race and Culture in Counseling and Psychotherapy* (1st ed.), by J. E. Helms and D. Cook, 1999, p. 90. Boston: Allyn & Bacon/Merrill Education. Copyright 1999 by Pearson Education. Reprinted with permission.

Appendix G

TABLE G.1 Summary of ALANA Racial Identity Ego Statuses, Examples, and Information-Processing Strategies (IPS)[a]

Status	Example
Conformity (Pre-encounter): External self-definition that implies devaluing of own group and allegiance to White standards of merit. Person probably is oblivious to socioracial groups' sociopolitical histories. IPS: Selective perception, distortion, minimization, and obliviousness to socioracial concerns.	Example: "If you are mixed race [Black-White] person, don't deny your European heritage just because Black people [in the United States] try to force you to choose. We are special because of our White heritage! We can be mediators of peace between these two warring peoples" (Helms & Cook, 1999, p. 87).
Dissonance (Encounter): Ambivalence and confusion concerning own socioracial group commitment and ambivalent socioracial self-definition. Person may be ambivalent about life decisions. IPS: Repression of anxiety-evoking racial information, ambivalence, anxiety, and disorientation.	Example: "I talked 'white,' moved 'white,' most of my friends were white. … But I never really felt accepted by or truly identified with the white kids. At some point, I stopped laughing when they would imitate Black people dancing. I distanced myself from the white kids, but I hadn't made an active effort to make black friends because I was never comfortable enough in my 'blackness' to associate with them. That left me in sort of a gray area" (Wenger, 1993, p. 4).
Immersion: Idealization of one's socioracial group and denigration of that which is perceived as White. Use of own-group external standards to self-define, and own-group commitment and loyalty is valued. May make life decisions for the benefit of the group. IPS: Hypervigilence and hypersensitivity toward racial stimuli and dichotomous thinking.	Example: "So there I was, strutting around with my semi-Afro, studiously garbling the English language because I thought that 'real' Black people didn't speak standard English, … contemplating changing my name to Malika, or something authentically Black" (Nelson, 1993, p. 18).
Emmersion: A euphoric sense of well-being and solidarity that accompanies being surrounded by people of one's own socioracial group. IPS: Uncritical of one's own group, peacefulness, and joyousness.	Example: "A jubilant [Black] scream went up … we had a feeling, and above all we had power. … So many whites unconsciously had never considered that blacks [sic] could do much of anything, least of all get a black candidate this close to being mayor of Chicago" (McClain, 1983, as cited in Helms, 1990, p. 25).
Internalization: Positive commitment to and acceptance of one's own socioracial group, internally defined racial attributes, and capacity to objectively assess and respond to members of the dominant group. Can make life decisions by assessing and integrating socioracial group requirements and self-assessment. IPS: Flexibility and abstraction.	Example: "By claiming myself as African-American and Black, I also inherit a right to ask questions about what this identity means. And chances are this identity will never be static, which is fine with me" (Jones, 1994, p. 78).

Continued

TABLE G.1 Summary of ALANA Racial Identity Ego Statuses, Examples, and Information-Processing Strategies (IPS)[a] (*Continued*)

Status	Example
Integrative Awareness: Capacity to value one's own collective identities as well as empathize and collaborate with members of other oppressed groups. Life decisions may be motivated by globally humanistic self-expression. IPS: Flexible and complex.	Example: "[I think of difference not] as something feared or exotic, but difference as one of the rich facts of one's life, a truism that gives you more data, more power and more flavor … [you need a variety of peoples in your life] … so you won't lapse into thinking you're God's gift to all knowledge as a North American Negro" (Jones, 1994, p. 80).

Note: Descriptions of racial identity statuses are adapted from Helms, J.E. (1994). Racial identity and other "racial" constructs. In E.J. Trickett, R. Watts, & D. Birman (Eds.)., *Human Diversity* (285–311). San Francisco: Jossey Bass. Statuses and are described in the order they are hypothesized to evolve.

[a] From *Using Race and Culture in Counseling and Psychotherapy* (1st ed.), by J. E. Helms and D. Cook, 1999, Boston: Allyn & Bacon/Merrill Education. Copyright 1999 by Pearson Education. Reprinted with permission.

OTHER RESOURCES

Music

- Putumayo series
- Lila Downs, *La Linea* (any of her other works)

Web Site

- http://www.soundjourney.com

References

American Counseling Association. (2005). *Ethics*. Retrieved May 26, 2008, from http://www.counseling.org/Resources/CodeOfEthics/TP/Home/CT2.aspx

Association for Specialists in Group Work. (2000). *Professional standards for the training of group workers*. Retrieved May 26, 2008, from http://www.asgw.org/training_standards.htm

Association for Specialists in Group Work. (1998). *Principles for diversity competent group workers*. Retrieved May 26, 2008, from http://www.asgw.org/diversity.htm

Bennis, W. G., & Shepard, H. A. (1970). A theory of group development. In Golembiewski, R. T., & Blumberg, A. (Eds.), *Sensitivity training and the laboratory approach: Readings about concepts and applications*. Itasca, IL: F.E. Peacock Publishers. pp. 91–115.

Bennis, W. G., & Shepard, H. A. (1956). A theory of group development. *Human Relations, 9*, 415–437.

Bion, W. R. (1961). *Experiences in groups*. New York: Basic Books.

Bowman, V. E. (1996). Counselor self-awareness and ethnic self-knowledge as a critical component of multicultural training. In J. L. DeLucia-Waack (Ed.), *Multicultural counseling competencies: Implications for training and practice*. Alexandria, VA: Association for Counselor Education and Supervision. pp. 7–30.

Bradford, L. P., Gibb, J. R., & Benne, K. D. (1964). *T-Group theory and laboratory method: Innovation in re-education*. New York: John Wiley & Sons.

Carter, L.F. (1953) On defining leadership. In M. Sherif and M.O. Wilson (Eds.), *Group Relations at the Crossroads*. New York: Harper, pp. 262–265.

Casas, J.M. (1984) Policy, training, and research in counseling psychology: The racial/ethnic minority perspective. In Brown, S.D., & Lent, R.W. (Eds.). *Handbook of counseling psychology*, New York: John Wiley, pp. 785–831.

Castaneda, C. (1972) *Journey to Ixtlan*, NY: Simon and Schuster.

Corey, G. (1991). *Theory and practice of counseling and psychotherapy* (4th ed.). Pacific Grove, CA: Brooks/Cole.

Corey, M. S., & Corey, G. (2006). *Groups process and practice* (7th ed.). Belmont, CA: Brooks/Cole.

Corey, M. S., & Corey, G. 1977). *Groups process and practice* (1st ed.). Belmont, CA: Brooks/Cole.

Corvin, S., & Wiggins, F. (1989). An antiracism training model for White professionals. *Journal of Multicultural Counseling and Development, 17*, 105–114.

Dass, R. (1971). *Be here now*. New York: Crown Publishing.

DeLucia-Waack, J. L. (1996). *Multicultural counseling competencies: Implications for training and practice*. Alexandria, VA: Association for Counselor Education and Supervision.

Donigian, J., & Malnati, R. (1997). *Systemic group therapy: A triadic model*. Pacific Grove, CA: Brooks/Cole.

Duke, L. (1994, August 28). This harrowed ground. *The Washington Post* Magazine, pp. 8–13; 20–25.

Durkin, H.E. (1981) *Living groups: Group psychotherapy and general systems theory*. New York: Brunner/Mazel (pp. 5–23).

Fisher, A.Q. (2001) *Finding Fish: A memoir*, NY: Harper Perennial.

Garland, J. A., Jones, H.E., & Kilodny, R. L. (1965). A model for stages of development in social work groups. In S. Bernstein. (Ed.). *Explorations in group work: Essays in theory and practice*. Boston: Boston University School of Social Work. pp. 12–53.

REFERENCES

Gibb, J. R. (1961). Defensive communication. *Journal of Communication, 11*, 141–148.

Gladding, S. T. (2001) *The counseling dictionary: Concise definitions of frequently used terms.* New Jersey: Prentice-Hall.

Glidewell, J. (1970). *Choice points: Essays on the emotional problems of living with people.* Cambridge: MIT press.

Golembiewski, R. T., & Blumberg, A. (Eds.) (1970), *Sensitivity training and the laboratory approach: Readings about concepts and applications.* Itasca, IL: F.E. Peacock Publishers.

Helms, J. E., & Cook, D. A. (1999). *Using race and culture in counseling and psychotherapy theory and process.* Needham Heights, MA: Allyn & Bacon.

Helms, J.E. (1994). Racial identity and other "racial" constructs. In E.J. Trickett, R. Watts, & D. Birman (Eds.)., *Human Diversity* San Francisco: Jossey Bass. pp. 285–311.

Helms, J.E. (Ed.). (1990). *Black and White racial identity: Theory, research, and practice.* Westport, CT: Greenwood Press.

Hill, N.R. (2003). Promoting and celebrating multicultural competence in counselor trainees. *Counselor Education and Supervision, 43*, 39–51.

Holcomb-McCoy, C., & Myers, J. (1999). Multicultural competence and counselor training: A national survey. *Journal of Counseling and Development, 77*, 294–302.

Hulse-Kilacky, D., Killacky, J., & Donigian, J. (2001). *Making task groups work in your world.* Upper Saddle River, NJ: Merrill/Prentice Hall.

Jackson, J.M. (1959) A space for conceptualizing person-group relationships. *Human Relations*, 12, 3–15.

Jones, L. (1994, May). Mama's White. *Essence Magazine*, pp.78, 80, 148.

Katz, J. H. (1978). *White awareness: Anti-racism training.* Norman: University of Oklahoma Press.

Kline, W. B. (2003). *Interactive group counseling and therapy.* Upper Saddle River, NJ: Merrill Prentice Hall.

Lewin, K. (1944). The dynamics of group action. *Educational Leadership, 1*, 195–200.

Lieberman, M.A., Yalom, I.D., Miles, M.B. (1973) *Encounter groups: First facts.* New York, NY: Basic Books.

Luft, J. (1969). *Of human interaction.* Palo Alto, CA: Mayfield Publishing.

Nelson, J. (1993). *Volunteer slavery: My authentic Negro experience.* Chicago: Noble Press.

Ochs, N.G. (1994). The incidence of racial issues in White counseling dyads: An exploratory survey. *Counselor Education and Supervision, 33*, 305–313.

Rank, O. *Will Therapy.* (1936 First published in English), New York, NY: reprinted in paperback by W.W. Norton Inc., 1978.

Rogers, C. R. (1970). *Carl Rogers on encounter groups.* New York: Harper & Row.

Rogers, Carl. (1969). *Freedom to Learn: A View of What Education Might Become.* (1st ed.) Columbus, Ohio: Charles Merill.

Rogers, C. R. (1961). *On becoming a person.* Boston: Houghton Mifflin.

Rogers, C.R. (1957). The necessary and sufficient conditions of therapeutic personality change. *Journal of consulting and clinical psychology* (Washington, DC), no. 21, p. 95–103.

Schutz, W. C. (1966). *The interpersonal underworld.* Palo Alto, CA: Science and Behavior Books.

Shakoor, M., & Rabinowicz, S. (1978). The sought membership model: A model for conceptualizing person-group relationships in groups where membership is sought. *Small Group Behavior, 3*, 325–329.

Sue, D.W. (1978) Eliminating cultural oppression in counseling: Toward a general theory. *Journal of counseling psychology*, 25, 419–428.

Sullivan, H. S. (1953) *The interpersonal theory of psychiatry.* New York: Norton.

Tolle, E. (1999) *The power of now*. Novato, CA: New World Library.
Tuckman, B.W. (1965). Development sequences in small groups. *Psychological Bulletin,* 63, 384–399.
U.S. Bureau of the Census. (1992). *Census of population and housing summary*. Washington, D.C.: U.S. Government Printing Office.
Wenger, J. (1993). Just part of the mix. *Focus, 21,* (9), 3–4.
Wheelan, S.A., Tsumura, E., & Kline, S.F. (1998) *Member perceptions of internal group dynamics and productivity*. Small Group Research, Vol 29, No. 3, 371–393.
Whitaker, D. S., & Lieberman, M. A. (1964). *Psychotherapy through the group process*. New York: Atherton Press.
Whitaker, D. S. (1989). Group focal conflict theory: Description, illustration and evaluation. *Group, 13,* 225–251.
Whitfield, D. (1994). Toward and integrated approach to improving multicultural counselor education. *Journal of Multicultural Counseling and Development, 22,* 239–252.
Williamson, E.G. (1939) *How to Counsel Students: A Manual of Techniques for Clinical Counselors*. New York: McGraw-Hill
Yalom, I. D. (1995). *The theory and practice of group psychotherapy* (4th ed.). New York: Basic Books.

SUGGESTED READING

Alexander, C. M., & Sussman, L. (1995). Creative approaches to multicultural counseling. In J. G. Ponterotto, J. M. Casas, L. A. Suzuki, & C. M. Alexander (Eds.), *Handbook of multicultural counseling*. Thousand Oaks, CA: Sage.
Allport, G. W. (1954). *The nature of prejudice*. Reading, MA: Addison-Wesley.
Anderson, D. (2007). Multicultural group work: A force for developing and healing. *Journal for Specialists in Group Work, 32*(3), 224–244.
Angelou, M. (1970). *I know why the caged bird sings*. New York: Random House.
Aponte, J. F., & Wohl, J. (2000). *Psychological intervention and cultural diversity* (2nd ed.) Needham Heights, MA: Allyn & Bacon.
Association for Multicultural Counseling and Development. (1996). *Multicultural counseling competencies and standards*. Retrieved May 26, 2008, from http://www.counseling.org/Resources/
Association for Specialists in Group Work. (2007). *Best practices*. Retrieved May 26, 2008, from http://www.asgw.org/PDF/Best_Practices.pdf
Atkinson, D. R., Morten, G., & Sue, D. W. (1989). *Counseling American minorities*. Dubuque, IA: William C. Brown.
Bates, M., Johnson, C. D., & Blaker, K. E. (1982). *Group leadership: A manual for group counseling leaders* (2nd ed.). Denver: Love.
Bemack, F., & Chi-Ying Chung, R. (2004). Teaching multicultural group counseling: Perspectives for a new era. *Journal for Specialists in Group Work, 29*(1), 31–42.
Benne, K. D., & Sheats, P. (1948). Functional roles of group members. *Journal of Social Issues, 2,* 42–47.
Bowen, M. (1966). The use of family therapy in clinical practice. *Comprehensive Psychiatry, 7,* 345–374.
Brown, D. A. (1970). *Bury my heart at Wounded Knee: An Indian history of the American West*. New York: H. Holt.
Capuzzi, D., & Gross, D. R. (Eds.). (1992). *Introduction to group counseling*. Denver: Love.

Carney, C. G., & Kahn, K. B. (1984). Building competencies for effective cross-cultural counseling: A developmental view. *The Counseling Psychologist, 12,* 111–119.

Carroll, M., Bates, M., & Johnson, C. (1997). *Group leadership: Strategies for group counseling leaders* (3rd ed.). Denver: Love.

Cartwright, D., & Zander, A. (1968). *Group dynamics: Research and theory* (3rd ed.). New York: Harper & Row.

Cheatham, H. E. (1991). *Cultural pluralism on campus.* Alexandria, VA: American College Personnel Association.

Conyne, R. K., Wilson, F. R., & Ward, D. E. (1997). *Comprehensive group work: What it means and how to teach it.* Alexandria, VA: American Counseling Association.

Cross, W. E. (1971). The Negro-to-Black conversion experience. *Black World, 20,* 13–27.

D'Andrea, M., & Daniels, J. (1991). Exploring the different levels of multicultural counseling training in counselor education. *Journal of Counseling and Development, 70,* 70–85.

D'Andrea, M., & Daniels, J. (1997). Multicultural group counseling. In S. T. Gladding (Ed.), *New developments in group counseling.* Greensboro, NC: ERIC Clearinghouse on Counseling and Student Services.

Dass, R., & Gorman, P. (1985). *How can I help?: Stories and reflections on service.* NewYork: Alfred A. Knopf.

Davidson, J. R. (1997). Experiential exercises for increasing self-awareness and an appreciation of racially and ethnically diverse populations. *Journal of Intergroup Relations, 24,* 22–33.

DeLucia-Waack, J. L., & Donigian, J. (2004). *The practice of multicultural group work: Visions and perspectives from the field.* Belmont, CA: Brooks/Cole.

Donigian, J., & Hulse-Killacky, D. (1999). *Critical incidents in group therapy* (2nd ed.). Belmont, CA: Brooks/Cole.

Dyer, W. G. (1972). *Modern theory and method in group training.* New York: Van Nostrand Reinhold.

Forsyth, D. R. (1990). *Group dynamics* (2nd ed.). Pacific Grove, CA: Brooks/Cole.

Freud, S. (1922). *Group psychology and the analysis of the ego.* London: Hogarth.

Fukuyama, M. A. (1990). Taking a universal approach to multicultural counseling. *Counselor Education and Supervision, 30,* 6–17.

Gibbard, G. S., Hartman, J. J., & Mann, R. D. (Eds.). (1974). *Analysis of groups.* San Francisco: Jossey-Bass.

Gladding, S. T. (1995). *Group work: A counseling specialty* (2nd ed.). Columbus, OH: Merrill.

Gladding, S. T. (1999). *Group work: A counseling specialty* (3rd ed.). Columbus, OH: Merrill.

Goldsmith, O. (1973). *Treasury of Aesop's fables.* New York: Crown Publishers.

Hall, C. S., & Lindzey, G. (1978). *Theories of personality* (3rd ed.). New York: John Wiley & Sons.

Hall, E. T. (1959). *The silent language.* New York: Doubleday.

Hall, E. T. (1966). *The hidden dimension.* New York: Doubleday.

Harvey, V., Geneva, D., & Hunter, W. J. (1975). A comparison of verbal and non-verbal groups. *Small Group Research, 6,* 210–219.

Helms, J. E. (1984). Toward a theoretical explanation of the effects of race on counseling: A Black and White model. *The Counseling Psychologist, 12,* 153–165.

Helms, J. E. (1993). *Black and White racial identity: Theory, research and practice.* Westport, CT: Praeger.

Homan, M. S. (2004). *Promoting community change: Making it happen in the real world* (3rd ed.). Belmont, CA: Brooks/Cole.

Hood, A. B., & Arceneaux, C. (1987). Multicultural counseling: Will what you don't know help you? *Counselor Education and Supervision, 26,* 173–175.

Howard-Hamilton, M., & Williams, V. A. (1993). Training and teaching cross-cultural issues: A flexible workshop model. *College Student Affairs Journal, 12,* 81–84.

Hulnick, H. R. (1977). Counselor: Know thyself. *Counselor Education and Supervision, 17,* 69–72.

Ibrahim, F. A., & Arredondo, P. M. (1986). Ethical standards for cross-cultural counseling: Counselor preparation, practice, assessment, and research. *Journal of Counseling and Development, 64,* 349–352.

Johnson, D. W., & Johnson, F. P. (2000). *Joining together: Group theory and group skills* (7th ed.). Boston: Allyn & Bacon.

Johnson, S. D. (1990). Toward clarifying culture, race, and ethnicity in the context of multicultural counseling. *Journal of Multicultural Counseling and Development, 18,* 41–50.

Kerner Commission. (1968). *National advisory commission on civil rights.* New York: Bantam.

Klein, R. H. (1996). Introduction to the special section on termination and group therapy. *International Journal of Group Psychotherapy, 46,* 1–4.

Kline, W. B. (1986). Working through the risks: A structured experience to facilitate self-disclosure. *Journal for Specialists in Group Work, 11,* (4) 209–212.

Kline, W. B. (1990). Responding to problem members. *Journal for Specialists in Group Work, 15,* (4) 195–200.

Kline, W. B. (1997). Group as a whole dynamics and the problem member: Conceptualization and intervention. In S. T. Gladding (Ed.), *New developments in group counseling.* Greensboro, NC: ERIC Clearinghouse on Counseling and Student Services. pp. 93–95.

Kottler, J. A. (1994). Working with difficult group members. *Journal for Specialists in Group Work, 19,* 3–10.

Lee, C. C. (1991). Promise and pitfalls of multicultural counseling. In C. C. Lee & B. L. Richardson (Eds.), *Multicultural issues in counseling: New approaches to diversity* (pp. 1–13). Alexandria, VA: American Association for Counseling and Development.

Locke, D. C. (1992). *Increasing multicultural understanding: A comprehensive model.* Newbury Park, CA: Sage.

Luft, J. (1970). *Group processes: An introduction to group dynamics* (2nd ed.). Palo Alto, CA: National Press Books.

McIntosh, P. (1989). White privilege: Unpacking the invisible knapsack. *Peace and Freedom,* (July/August). pp. 10–12. [Newsletter]

Meier, S. T., & Davis, S. R. (1997). *The elements of counseling* (3rd ed.). Pacific Grove, CA: Brooks/Cole.

Midgette, T. E., & Meggert, S. S. (1991). Multicultural counseling instruction: A challenge for faculties in the 21st century. *Journal of Counseling and Development, 70,* 136–141.

Minuchin, S. (1974). *Families and family therapy.* Cambridge, MA: Harvard University Press.

Parham, T. A. (1989). Cycles of psychological nigrescence. *The Counseling Psychologist, 17,* 187–226.

Parr, G., Haberstroh, S., & Kotler, J. (2000). Interactive journal writing as an adjunct in group work. *Journal for Specialists in Group Work, 25*(3), 229–242.

Pedersen, P. (1988). *A handbook for developing multicultural awareness.* Alexandria, VA: American Association for Counseling and Development.

Pederson, P. B. (1991). Multiculturalism as a generic approach to counseling. *Journal of Counseling and Development, 70,* 6–12.

Pfeiffer, J. W., & Jones, J. E. (1971). *A handbook of structured experiences for human relations training* (Vols. 1–3). Iowa City, IA: University Associates Press.

Ponterotto, J. G. (1988). Racial consciousness development among White counselor trainees: A stage model. *Journal of Multicultural Counseling and Development, 66,* 237–241.

Ponterotto, J. G., Casas, J. M., Suzuki, L. A., & Alexander, C. M. (1995). *Handbook of multicultural counseling.* Thousand Oaks, CA: Sage.

Ponterotto, J. G., Casas, J. M., Suzuki, L. A., & Alexander, C. M. (2001). *Handbook of multicultural counseling* (2nd ed.). Thousand Oaks, CA: Sage.

Preli, R., & Bernard, J. M. (1993). Making multiculturalism relevant for majority culture graduate students. *Journal of Marital and Family Therapy, 19,* 5–16.

Rice, P. F. (1990). *Intimate relationships, marriages and families.* Mountain View, CA: Mayfield Publishing.

Ruiz, P. M. (2001). *The four agreements: A practical guide to personal freedom, a Toltec wisdom book.* San Rafael, CA: Amber-Allen Publishing.

Schutz, W.C. (1973) *Elements of encounter.* Big Sur, California: Joy Press

Sedwick, R. C. (1974). *Interaction: Interpersonal relationships in organizations.* Englewood Cliffs, NJ: Prentice Hall.

Shakoor, M. (2004a). A member leaves the group. In R. Perusse, J. Whitledge, & L. Tyson (Eds.), *Critical incidents in group work.* American Counseling Association. pp. 21–26.

Shakoor, M. (2004c). Multicultural group work: A transpersonal Afro-centric perspective (Cultural, Social, and Family Autobiographies. In J. L. DeLucia-Waack & J. Donigian (Eds.), *The practice of multicultural group work: Eleven visions.* Pacific Grove, CA: Brooks-Cole. pp. 80–83.

Shakoor, M. (2004d). Psycho-educational group vignette #1: The first meeting and group silence. In J. L. DeLucia-Waack & J. Donigian (Eds.), *The practice of multicultural group work: Eleven visions.* Pacific Grove, CA: Brooks-Cole. pp. 151–158.

Shakoor, M. (2004b). Counseling/therapy group vignette #1: The assertiveness group and the bomb. In J. L. DeLucia-Waack & J. Donigian (Eds.), *The practice of multicultural group work: Eleven visions.* Pacific Grove, CA: Brooks-Cole. pp. 205–214.

Shakoor, M., & Fister, D. L. (2000). Finding hope in Bosnia: Fostering resilience through group process intervention. *Journal for Specialists in Group Work, 25*(3), 269–287.

Shakoor, M., & Tanner, W. L. (1978). Organization development at the grass roots: First-line management team building in a public housing project. In R. Golembiewski (Ed.), *Organization development in public administration: Public sector applications of organization development technology* (pp. 297–311). New York: Marcel Dekker.

Shakoor, M. A. (1973). *The process consultant as system's interventionist with an internal planning team.* Unpublished doctoral dissertation, Kent State University, Kent, OH.

Shepherd, C. R. (1964). *Small groups: Some sociological perspectives.* Scranton, PA: Chandler Publishing.

Speight, S. L., Myers, L. J., Cox, C. E., & Highlen, P. S. (1991). A redefinition of multicultural counseling. *Journal of Counseling and Development, 70,* 29–36.

Stock, D., & Lieberman, M. A. (1958). The deviant member in therapy groups. *Human Relations, 11,* 341–372.

Sue, D., Bernier, J., Durran, A., Feinbeg, L., Pedersen, P., Smith, E., et al. (1982). Position paper: Cross-cultural counseling competencies. *The Counseling Psychologist, 10,* 45–52.

Sue, D. W., & Sue, D. (1990). *Counseling the culturally different: Theory and practice.* (2nd Ed.). New York: John Wiley & Sons.

Tan, A. (1989). *The joy luck club.* New York: J. P. Putnam and Sons.

Tyson, L. E., Perusse, R., & Whitledge, J. (2004). *Critical incidents in group counseling.* Alexandria, VA: American Counseling Association.

Vander Kolk, C. J. (1985). *Introduction to group counseling and psychotherapy*. Columbus, OH: Merrill.
Walker, A. (1982). *The color purple*. New York: Harcourt, Brace, Jovanovich.
Whitaker, D. S. (1985). *Using groups to help people*. London: Routledge.
Yalom, I. D. (1970). *The theory and practice of group psychotherapy*. New York: Basic Books.
Yalom, I. D. (1975). *The theory and practice of group psychotherapy* (2nd ed.). New York: Basic Books.

Index

A

Acceptance, xxxv, 87
Acknowledgment, xxi
Advice giving, xxxv
ALANA (African Americans, Latinos, Asians, and Native Americans), xxxv, 107, 113–114
Alertness, 42
Ambiguity, xx–xxi, xxxv
Anxiety, xxxv, 7, 8, 21
Apprentice, xxv, 18, 58, 80–81
Ascribed identity, 108
Assessment
    of attitude, xv–xvii, 16–17, 36–37, 79–80
    of self, 21
Association for Specialists in Group Work (ASGW), 2
Atmosphere, xxxv
Attack on the leader, xxxvi
Attitude
    assessment of your, xv–xvii, 16–17, 36–37, 79–80
    facilitative, xvi
    nonfacilitative, xvi
Attraction, xxxvi, 87
Authoritarian leaders, xxxvi
Authority, xxiii, xxxvi, 8–9
Autonomy, 112
Avoidance, 19
Awareness
    diversity, 2
    self, xxx, xxxii–xxxiii, xli, 3–4

B

Beginning stage, 7–18
    characteristics of, 7–8
    group challenges in, 8–9
    member challenges in, 7, 9
    multicultural considerations, 14–15
    review questions, 15–16
    scenarios, 10–15
    tips for, 16–18
Be Here Now, xxvi–xxvii
Biracial identity, 108
Black racial identity theories, xxxvi
Body language, xxxvi, 8
Boundaries
    defined, xxxvi
    group, xiv
    violations of, 19

Boundarying, xiv
Bowman's mode of self-awareness, 3–4

C

Caring, 87
Castaneda, Carlos, xxv
Catharsis, xxxvi, 96
Change, xxi, 62–63
Change space, 88
Clarity, 17–18
Climate, xxxvi, 40
Closeness, 8–9, 41
Cognitive mechanics, xxx
Collaboration, xxxvii
Communication, effective, xxvii
Confidentiality, xiv, 97
Conflict, xxiii–xxiv, 19–21, 34–35, 39, 58
Conformity, 113
Confrontation, xxiii–xxiv, 34–35, 58
Congruence, xxiv, xxxvii
Consensual validation, xxxvii
Constructive openness, xvii, xix
Contact, 111
Content, xxii–xxiii, xxxvii, 18, 35–36, 58, 78
Corrective recapitulation of the primary family group, xxxvii
Counseling, xxxvii
Counterdependence, 19
Counterpersonals, 20–21
Credentials, 95–96
Cultural diversity, 2
Curative factors, xxxvii

D

Dass, Ram, xxvii
Democratic leaders, xxxvii
Dependency, xxvii–xxxviii
Disclosure, xxxviii
Discomfort, 17–18
Disenchantment, 40–41
Disintegration, 111
Dissonance, 113
Disturbing motives, xxxviii, 103
Diversity awareness, 2
Dyad, xxxviii
Dynamics, xx–xxii, xxxviii

E

Early middle stage, 19–37
    characteristics of, 19–20

group challenges in, 20–21
member challenges in, 19, 21–22
multicultural considerations, 31–34
review questions, 34
scenarios, 22–34
tips for, 34–37
Ego statuses, 109, 111–114
Emersion, 112, 113
Emotional intensity, 40, 41
Emotional stimulation, 87
Emotional wiring, xxx
Empathize, xxxviii
Empathy, xxiv
Enabling solution, xxxviii
Enabling solutions, 104
Enchantment, 40
Ending stage (termination), 61–81
characteristics of, 61–62
group challenges in, 62–63
member challenges in, 61, 63
multicultural considerations, 74–77
review questions, 77–78
scenarios, 63–77
tips for, 78–81
Ethical concerns, 95–97
Ethnic groups, 4
Ethnicity, xxxviii
Executive function, 87
Exit space, 88
Expectations
about group leader, 84
about safety, xiv, 36
Experiential, xxxviii
Experiential learning, xx, 4, 17

F

Facilitative attitude, xvi
Factions, 19–20
Family wounds, 63
Fear, disempowering, xx–xxi
Feedback, xiv, xvii, xxviii–xxix, xxxviii–xxxix, 39–40
Feelings, expression of, xxix
Flight, 19
Focal conflict theory, xxxix, 41, 103, 104
Frames of reference, 2–3
Freedom, xiv

G

Group challenges
in beginning stage, 8–9
in early middle stage, 20–21
in ending stage, 62–63
in late middle stage, 40–41
Group cohesiveness, xxxix
Group collusion, xxxix

Group counseling, xxxix
Group culture, xxxix
Group development stages
beginning stage, 7–18
early middle stage, 19–37
ending stage, 61–81
introduction to, 1–2
late middle stage, 39–59
Group dynamics, xx–xxii, xxxix
Group leaders/leadership, 83–94
credentials of, 95–96
dependence on, 19
expectations about, 84
functions of, 86, 87
responsibilities of, 9
sought membership model and, 85–87
Group member challenges
in beginning stage, 7, 9
in early middle stage, 19, 21–22
in ending stage, 61, 63
in late middle stage, 39, 42
Group member guide sheet, 99
Group members
bonds between, 20
counterpersonals, 20–21
effective mindset for, xiii–xxv, 34–35, 57–58, 78
independent, 20, 22
personals, 20
relationships with, xxiv–xxv
silent, xxx
strategies and skills for success in, 37, 81
as teachers, xx
Group norms, 85–86
Group process, xxx
Group psychotherapy, xxxix
Group relations, 87–88
Groups
effective, xi
fragmentation of, 19–20
strategies and skills for success in, xxv–xxxiv, 18, 59
as three-element system, xx–xxii
understanding purpose of, xiii–xiv, 16, 36, 79
Group scenarios, 4–5
beginning stage, 10–15
early middle stage, 22–34
ending stage, 63–77
late middle stage, 42–57
leadership function, 88–94
Group solutions, xxxix, 103–105
Group therapy, xxxix
Group think, 95
Group work
initiating in, xxix–xxx
interactive processes of, xx–xxii, 18, 35, 57–58, 78

Group-work apprentice, xxv, 18, 58, 80–81
Growth
 engendering, 58, 80
 transformative, xix

H

Helms, J. E., 107–108
Homeostasis, xxxix

I

Immersion, 111, 113
Inappropriate catharsis, 96
Independents, 20, 22
Information flow, boundaries of, xiv
Information-processing strategies (IPS), 111–112, 113–114
Initiating, xxix–xxx
Integration, xxv, 80
Integrative awareness, 114
Integrity, 97
Intention, xxxiii
Intentionality, xxxiii
Intentions, 95
Interactive processes, of group work, xx–xxii, 18, 35, 57–58, 78
Internalization, 113
Interpersonal, xxxix
Interpersonal conflict, xxiii
Interpersonal issues, xxii, 35
Intervention, xxxix
Intimacy, xxiii, 41
Intrapersonal, xxxix
Intrapersonal conflict, xxiii

J

Johari Window, xvii–xx
Journals, xxxi–xxxii

L

Late middle stage, 39–59
 characteristics of, 39–40
 group challenges in, 40–41
 member challenges in, 39, 42
 multicultural considerations, 53–57
 review questions, 57
 scenarios, 42–57
 tips for, 57–59
Leaders/leadership, 83–94
 credentials of, 95–96
 defined, 83–84
 expectations about, 84
 functions, 86, 87
 scenarios, 88–94
 sought membership model and, 85–87

Learning, experiential, xx, 4, 17
Listening, xxvii
Loss, 63
Luft, Joseph, xvii–xx

M

Marginal identity, 108
Mastery, xxv
Meaning attribution, 87
Member mindset, key components of effective, xiii–xxv, 34–35, 57–58, 78
Membership, xl
Methods, 8
Minority groups, 2
Monoracial identity, 108
Motivations, 95
Multicultural considerations
 beginning stage, 14–15
 early middle stage, 31–34
 ending stage, 74–77
 late middle stage, 53–57
Multicultural diversity, 2
Multicultural groups, 3
Multicultural resources, 101–102
Multicultural training, 3–4

N

Negative attraction, 87
Nonfacilitative attitude, xvi
Norms, xl, 85–86
Noticing, xxi

O

Openness, xvii, xix
Ownership, xl

P

Parataxic distortion, xl
Participation
 mandated, xv
 three lenses approach to, xxx–xxxi
Personal change, xxi
Personal evaluation, xxviii
Personal experiences, recording, xxxi–xxxii
Personal identity, 107
Personal process, xxx, 96
Personals, 20
Personal values, 96
Perspectives, dynamic, xxx–xxxi
POC (People of Color), xl
Positive acceptance, 87
Positive attraction, 87
Power, 8–9
Power field, 86

Preference group relation, 88
Process
 awareness of, xxx
 vs. content, xxii–xxiii, 18, 35–36, 58, 78
 defined, xl
 facilitation of, xxxii
 group, xxx
 personal, xxx, 96
Pseudo-independence, 111
Psychoeducational group, xl
Purpose, of group, xiii–xiv, 16, 36, 79

Q

Questions, xxvii–xxviii

R

Race, xl
Racial groups, 4
Racial identity, xl, 107–108, 111–114
Racial identity development theory, xl–xli
Racial identity models, 109
Reactive motives, xli, 103
Rebellion relation, 88
Reference group orientation, 108
Reference group relation, 87–88
Reflection, xxvii–xxviii, xxxii
Reintegration, 111
Relationships, with other group members, xxiv–xxv
Remembering, xxxii–xxxiii
Respect, expectations about, xiv
Restrictive solutions, xli, 104
Risk-taking, xli
Rogers, Carl, xxi

S

Safety expectations, xiv, 36
Self
 concept of, xi
 learning about, 3–4
Self-assessment, 21
Self-awareness, xxx, xxxii–xxxiii, xli, 3–4
Self-disclosure, xvii, 40

Self-discovery, 17, 37, 78–79
Self-exploration, xvi
Self-knowledge, 3–4
Silent members, xxx
Small groups, defined, xiii
Solutional conflict, xli, 104–105
Sought membership, 83
 acceptance and, 87
 concept of, 85
 concept of attraction, 87
 model, 85–86
Stereotypes, 4
Structure, need for, xx
Subgrouping, xiv
Sustain, 20
Synergy, xli
Systems theory, xli

T

Termination, see Ending stage (termination)
Themes, xli
Therapy, xli
Three lenses approach, xxx–xxxi
Transformative growth, xix
Transition, 62–63

U

Uncertainty, xx–xxi, 17–18, 61
Unconditional positive regard, xxiv–xxv
Understanding, xxxii
United States, cultural composition of, 2

V

Values, 96
VREG (visible racial ethnic group), xli

W

White culture, 4
White racial identity theories, xli–xlii, 111–112
Willingness, xxi
Work, xlii
Worldview, xlii, 2–3